THE FORCES BEHIND FENG SHUI
A Companion to Energizing Your Life

DAWN HANKINS

Library and Archives Canada Cataloguing in Publication

ISBN 978-0-9781145-9-6

IMNALA ⚬⁄ GROUP

To order, visit: www.imnalagroup.ca
Email: dawn.hankins@imnalagroup.ca
Telephone: (403) 619-1812

The author does not dispense medical advice or advocate the use of any technique as a form of treatment for physical or medical problems without the advice of a physician. The intent of the author is to offer general information to help readers in their quest for emotional and spiritual well-being. The author assumes no responsibility for readers' actions.

ATOM Art, Design and Illustration
atouchofmustard@gmail.com
All art and design by Johann Kyser, including cover, illustrations, and photographs, except:

Page 69: Stress - stock image
Pages 80, 86: Crystal & Bagua Mirror - Maureen Johnson
Pages 84, 85, 87: Puppies, Water on Stick and Kite - Ross Merritt, www.rossmerrittphotography.co.uk
Page 93: Front Door - Jenn Quint
Page 101: Bed - Laura Vanhoutte
Page 148: Author - Maureen Bissanti

Table of Contents

This Book is Dedicated to My Parents
Ronald John Simonds and Olive Decia Grace Simonds

Daffodils (1804)

I wandered lonely as a cloud
That floats on high o'er vales and hills
When all at once I saw a crowd
A host of golden daffodils
Beside the lake, beneath the trees
Fluttering and dancing in the breeze

Continuous as the stars that shine
And twinkle on the Milky Way
They stretch'd in never-ending line
Along the margin of a bay
Ten thousand saw I at a glance
Tossing their heads in sprightly dance

The waves beside them danced; but they
Out-did the sparkling waves in glee
A poet could not but be gay
In such a jocund company
I gazed -- and gazed -- but little thought
What wealth the show to me had brought

For oft, when on my couch I lie
In vacant or in pensive mood
They flash upon that inward eye
Which is the bliss of solitude
And then my heart with pleasure fills
And dances with the daffodils

By William Wordsworth (1770-1850)

Acknowledgements

To my friends who guided me on this path: His Holiness Grandmaster Professor Lin Yun, Her Holiness Crystal Chu Rinpoche, Eileen Weklar, Katherine Metz, Marina Lighthouse, Catherine Dawson-Laframboise, Debra Ford, Tanja Hale, Sandy Day, Marilyn Viccars, Maureen Johnson and everyone at Feng Shui Connections.

I would like to thank my husband John for his love and extensive support and encouragement throughout my Feng Shui history; my three beautiful daughters Lauren, Naomi and Imogen; and my family whose love fills my heart and soul, parents Ronald and Decia, siblings Richard, Barbara, Robert, Wendy and David, and parents-in-law Sylvia and Derek.

A special thank you to my editor, Fran Kimmel, for her help in the writing of this book.

Preface

What dreams did you have as a child? Did you want to become a superstar? A famous singer perhaps or an actor? Did you ever imagine your life as it is now?

My life has taken a much different path than I dreamed about as a child. I started out wanting to be a ballet dancer but something seemed to hold me back. I was very easily influenced by my teachers, family and friends and would often pursue what they wanted of me rather than chase my own dreams. I believe they wished me well and I am not suggesting that their intentions were wrong; however we have to follow our own dance in life and find the path to fulfill our own dreams and desires.

I've since learned that I have the power to attract good things into my world and that my life does not need to be such a struggle. True, I have not become a ballet dancer, but I have enjoyed the dances with the force behind Feng Shui. It is not always an easy path to the dance floor yet what I have discovered is that once you get your dancing shoes on, and put one foot in front of the other, it's amazing how all the obstacles appear to fall away. As Lao Tzu gently reminds us "The journey of a thousand miles begins with one step."

I think I've always felt the need to have balance around me. Without realizing it I have been practising aspects of Feng Shui since I was a child, carefully placing my teddy bears and Barbie dolls in neat rows on my bed, hanging my clothes in a certain way and ensuring that I wear nothing out of order. By understanding the forces of Feng Shui, you might recognise that you, too, have unconsciously been practising Feng Shui principles.

Is it time to discover your full potential? Are you ready to hit the dance floor to either learn a new dance or improve your current dance steps? Let's begin exploring what you really want from this life and how Feng Shui can help show you the way.

The Chi of Wealth

Don't assume that seeking wealth
is the same as being greedy

Money just may bring relief
in hard times when you're needy

Yet, if it is acquired and used
without a proper method

It'll be easier to capsize a boat
than to carry it afloat

Poem by His Holiness
Grandmaster Professor Lin Yun

Foreword by His Holiness
Grandmaster Professor Lin Yun

The Forces Behind Feng Shui: A Companion to Energizing Your Life by Dawn Hankins is another one of those books that I love, which introduces the strong and powerful force behind feng shui, and which enables your life to receive support and strength. The author is tireless in her studies; my relationship to her is as a teacher as well as a friend, and she has also taken refuge with me as a formal disciple. In clear and simple words, this book expounds the importance of feng shui, and explains in realistic detail about the yin-yang, the five elements, the eight trigrams, and how each trigram is centered in ch'i. This book certainly is beneficial to the families of those readers with good luck, good karma, and good heart.

This book introduces transcendental and mundane solutions, and the most secretive of Black Sect Tantric Buddhism's not-to-be-openly-shared "Methods of Minor Adjustments." The book also reminds readers not to neglect the three major chi fields in the house: (1) front door, (2) bedroom, and (3) kitchen. Finally this book provides many valuable case studies from feng shui consultations. There is a saying that one should "do one good deed per day." After reading this book, I feel it has the merits of having done ten good deeds per day. This is why Her Holiness Crystal Chu Rinpoche, the Successor of Black Sect Tantric Buddhism, has asked me to write this foreword before embarking on a long stay in Taiwan. I am happy to accept this bidding, and wish to bestow my blessings upon the author, readers, and their family members, and may they receive auspiciousness, longevity, wealth, health and safety.

> Those who view this will have ease;
> Those who recite this will have safety;
> Those who receive this will have good fortune;
> Those who keep this will have longevity.

> The Buddha assists those with karma.

Written on the fifth day of the Lunar May in the Ji-Chou year, at the request of Her Holiness Black Sect Tantric Buddhism Successor Crystal Chu Rinpoche. Having bathed, offered incense, and chanted infinite mantras, this was written to offer blessing to the author Dawn Hankins, her readers, and their families, for auspiciousness, wealth, good health, and safety.

Black Sect Tantric Buddhism
The Master of Yun Lin Temple,
Lin Yun Monastery, and Taipei Yun Shi Jing She

Lin Yun

At the time a visitor at Zi Hong Hall, the study of Crystal Rinpoche
(Translated from Chinese into English by Mary Hsu)

己丑端陽承女法王黑教再傳人筧立仁波切雜屬
沐浴焚香持無量咒以為本書作者

暨讀者闔府長幼祈福納吉進財保康宜了

DAWN
HANKINS

觀者順念者安得者福存者壽

佛門崇黑教第一廟雲林禪寺
佛堂台灣總舍
第三廟林豐禪院

寺禪院主人
時客之筧立
常虹軒

XV

Chapter 1.
Why Feng Shui?

Feng Shui (pronounced fung shway) is the art of balancing the flow of Chi in our surroundings to create beneficial effects in our lives. The force behind Feng Shui is very powerful. By making a few changes in our space, we can create an abundance of happiness we might not have thought possible.

We are all looking for what is missing in our lives. In my experience, there are three things that people usually want to change or improve. These include health, wealth and happiness. Think about it. If any of these three are seriously out of balance, it becomes that much harder to reach our full potential.

Without overall health, for example, nothing is possible. By maintaining or improving our general health, we automatically improve our state of mind, which gives us a better sense of balance in our lives.

And while money can't buy happiness, a true lack of money makes it hard to concentrate on improving our lives in other ways. Who hasn't dreamed about winning the lottery or earning more money for the good things in life? Whether we want to buy a dream home or pay for our children's education, a personal sense of wealth is important to most of us.

We will all define happiness a little differently. You might be looking to attract that special partner in your life or to ignite the embers of an existing relationship. Or you might want to improve relationships with your family, friends and co-workers or learn to trust in others again. For many of us happiness is connected to meaningful work. Perhaps you are looking for a new career direction or a different job in your current field, one that allows you to make a difference by using your skills and talents. Maybe you want your business to really take off.

Feng Shui is not a "fix all" but rather a method for you to take control and responsibility for your life and well-being. This book shows how small changes can result in big payoffs. Before you know it you can start living the life of your dreams.

Chapter 2.
A Step Back to the Beginning

Feng Shui has been with us for a very long time - 3,000 to 4,000 years in fact. Since its inception, Feng Shui has spread around the world. Over the years, we've seen its beliefs and customs alter so as to blend in with different cultures. The original writings of Feng Shui have been preserved by generations of masters in ancient China. This writing, which has been interpreted by all cultures, covers aspects of life from health and exercise, to personal relationships, to medicine and arts. Despite being driven underground many times by people who fear change, Feng Shui continues to transform lives today around the globe.

Literally translated, Feng Shui means Wind and Water and originates from China. The Chinese were the first to make the connection between surroundings and personal Chi. Early Chinese philosophers began to understand that when people balanced the Chi around them, they could bring harmony into their lives to achieve greater life success.

When it comes to the significance of the Feng Shui words we only have to think about our bodies. During the course of our day we inhale and exhale many times our own volume of "Feng" which is air. Approximately 70% of our body weight is made up of water which is "Shui". If we do not breathe then we will die within minutes. If we have no water to drink then we would surely perish within days. Nothing is more essential to us than air and water.

Both air and water carry the life Chi. They also comprise the bulk of the ecosystem on the surface of this planet. All around us, as well as within us, we are immersed in Feng Shui. We breathe from an abundance of air (the atmosphere), and we are reliant on a supply of fresh water to drink.

There are different schools to Feng Shui such as Form, Compass and various Taoist schools. While applications might be slightly different, the same core Feng Shui principles apply to every school of thought.

Black Sect Tantric Buddhism (BTB) is a relatively new movement originating about 40 years ago in California with Professor Lin Yun. The Professor, whose family was native to Taichung, Taiwan, was born and raised in Beijing. He began his studies with Lama Da-De at Yong-He Palace at the age of six years.

The Professor has shared his story of how his journey began. As a young six-year-old, he and some of his friends enjoyed playing very close to the Temple. One day, a monk came out and asked the boys if they would like to receive their teachings. While his friends ran away in fear, the Professor decided to stay.

After eleven years of study, the Professor then continued his studies and meditation in Taiwan with the great masters of BTB, Master Hui, Chieh-fu and Master Cheng, Kwei-ying until he attained a highly enlightened level of spiritual insights and incredible gifts. He then came to live in North America and began lecturing on the principals of BTB Feng Shui. He soon discovered his teachings from China did not compliment our culture as our land layout and customs were very different. To make Feng Shui more meaningful here in the West, Professor Lin Yun devised a new way of understanding BTB. He shows us that by combining contemporary and traditional knowledge, we can make modern living spaces harmonious in a way that is very easily understood. BTB derives, in part, from Indian and Tibetan Buddhist beliefs. By focusing on beliefs or religion and applying intentions in a positive and constructive way, we can create a favourable outcome.

The Professor's teachings differ from the more traditional methods in that he has placed a strong focus on the spiritual aspect, while incorporating contemporary methods and the theory of Chi (or energy).

I feel grateful and blessed to have had the privilege to study with HH Grandmaster Professor Lin Yun. The ideas shared in this book rely on BTB teachings.

His Holiness Grandmaster Professor Lin Yun and Dawn Hankins

Chapter 3.
What Do We Mean By Chi?

In Feng Shui, we use techniques or cures to control or influence the effects of Chi moving around a space. Chi means life force and is in absolutely everything around us. We cannot see Chi but we can certainly feel it in our mood shifts and daily experiences.

Think of a cell, which is regarded as the smallest unit of life. A cell responds to changes in its environment in order to exist, produce and die. If we accept that a cell has the ability to analyse a particular environment and produce any necessary cells or cures needed to balance, then it becomes quite feasible to see the universe as providing a print out of our lives, every second of the day. Just look around you. By talking with a person and then taking a look at their living environment, you can quickly assess if the two are in balance. This is what a true Feng Shui consultant will do during a consultation.[1]

Feelings, thoughts and past events have a very strong Chi. This Chi is closely intertwined with our own personal Chi. We cannot destroy Chi once it has been created, but we need to realize that every place, every person and every possession is connected by Chi. These energies evoke feelings of how we felt about these places, about the people we have met along the way, and about the things we bring back with us.

Think about how Chi works in your life. Are you the same person at work as you are at home or when out with your friends? I have delivered many workshops, and I watch with great interest to see how participants' Chi changes as workshops unfold. Participants almost always become more relaxed and more open. Why is that? Their Chi is adapting to the environment.

---

1. The Feng Shui Institute:
   http://www.feng-shui-institute.org/fengshuiscience.htm

Experience the Chi

Try these two simple exercises to get a sense of how Chi works.

First, rub your hands together for about 20 to 30 seconds; then part your hands slowly. You should feel like you are holding a balloon. Feel the pressure between your hands as you gently move them in and out.

For this next exercise you will need a coat hanger and a partner. To begin, stand about 20 feet from your partner. Ask your partner to just relax.

Using one hand, hold the wire coat hanger vertically at chest height with the hook facing toward your partner with the open end turned up. Hold the hanger very loosely by the long side of the triangle.

Begin walking slowly towards your partner continuing to hold the coat hanger very loosely.

Notice when the hanger begins to move left or right as you approach your partner. You are now meeting your partner's Chi field. Ask your partner to remember a time when he or she felt happy. Repeat again, this time remembering an angry or sad time. Notice the change in the Chi field.

Repeat this exercise using your pet as your partner. How strong is your pet's Chi field? You can even try this exercise independently, using a large mirror instead of a partner.

Freeing the Chi of Change

You've undoubtedly heard the saying that change is the only constant in our lives. Nothing stays the same. The same holds true for Chi, which is also constantly changing. When we understand and appreciate this, change becomes a gift that we can use to improve our lives.

How many of us find ourselves resisting change in the moment - It was so much better before! - only to later realize that the change itself helped us to grow. Once you embrace change you will notice its effects in your home and your life. You will find that your life appears to open up to new opportunities and that you are better able to adapt to life's needs.

However, you don't just have to sit back and wait for change or let change creep up on you. Ideally, you want to be in control of the dance to achieve your goals. A great way to evoke a change in your life is to move 27 things in your home. When you reposition items with an intention to make positive outcomes, you can shift the forces of Feng Shui towards your desired direction. By evoking the forces of Feng Shui, you allow your environment to evolve with you.

The Flow of Chi

If Chi is not flowing well, we can easily determine the state of the flow of Chi as we feel blocked, unhealthy and unhappy. When Chi is flowing gently, we feel happy, creative and successful.

Picture that dance floor. You glide along effortlessly listening to the beat and gentle tones of the orchestra of your life. With the use of Feng Shui techniques, we are able to create this flow of Chi. In turn this leads to a better balance and provides an environment that is nourishing and supportive for all who share the space. By making simple changes - whether in your home, your car or your workspace - you can attract your desires for better happiness, wealth, health and relationships.

Chapter 4.
Yin and Yang

Important components of Feng Shui are the yin and yang. Everything in life is ever changing and has an opposite - night and day, good and bad, hot and cold. Chi, too, works in opposites. The yin and yang are two opposing, yet complementary energies; both are necessary for a balanced life.

Yin Chi represents the passive side of nature, which is dark, whereas yang Chi represents the active side, which is light. With the use of Feng Shui tools, we are able to manipulate these two energies into balance, which in turn can improve life success.

Yin	Yang
Dark	Light
Female	Male
Passive	Active
Moon	Sun
Rain	Sunshine
Odd Numbers	Even Numbers
Winter	Summer
Introvert	Extrovert

Look closely at this yin and yang symbol and think about what you see and what it might mean.

Notice the two opposite spots and how both sides are exactly the same size and shape. Yin and yang represent male and female and this symbol shows us that nothing is purely one or the other. In other words, there is always a little of yang in yin and yin in yang.

We see constant reminders of the give and take of these energies in our daily lives. Even in our darkest times, there is always a light or a ray of hope at the end of the tunnel. Likewise, a little darkness can creep into our happiest moments as we ask ourselves questions like, "Will it last?" or "What happens if?"

Like everything in life, our physical surroundings contain both yin and yang energies. Creating a home that will reflect an appropriate yin yang balance is very important to overall well-being. With simple changes, you can do much to make this happen.

If a room in your home is too dark, for example, you can intentionally add light, which works to bring more yang Chi into the room, providing balance. This simple example of shifting Chi balance is called "applying a cure," a topic we will discuss in depth in a later chapter.

Creating Balance from the Inside Out

Yin and yang cannot only be balanced in your physical space, but also in your mind and body. It is quite common here in the West to spend considerable time working on our careers, struggling to achieve greatness and improve on our last achievement. We can spend so much time focusing our Chi on this area that our social and recreational time with families and friends start to suffer. Over time, relationships can be strained to the breaking point, and we end up destroying the very thing that we most want to improve![2]

---

2. There is an excellent section about yin and yang balance in the Feng Shui Bible, written by Simon Brown.

Look at these descriptors and ask yourself, "Which one am I?" Do you recognise any of these traits in yourself?

YIN PROMINENCE

Emotional - Prone to Sadness Fatigued - Tire easily Passive - Vulnerable Afflicted by Illness	For Better Balance, Add Yang: Wear Bright Yang Colours De-Clutter Your Space Exercise – Start a New Activity

YANG PROMINENCE

Anxious - Stressed Frustration - Anger Dominating - Controlling Tense - Uptight	For Better Balance, Add Yin: Meditate - Dream Commune with Nature - Take a walk, listen to relaxing music

A fast-paced stressful life must incorporate enough calming yin to help your body cope with all the activity. Alternately, you need enough radiant yang Chi to stay energized and transform essential nutrients. Everyone's balance is different, so it's important to find out what works for you.

Yin and Yang in the Forces of Nature

There are various ways of interpreting yin and yang, but I like to study the forces of nature itself.

How would your life prosper if you lived in a desert? A desert is heavily yin, the hot sun baking the earth. Here it's difficult to get sufficient water or fertile soil. Do you see yourself struggling or thriving in an environment such as this?

Perhaps a yang mountain environment would suit you better. Think of the shadowy crevices, the cold, snowy peaks, and the deafening quiet.

Maybe you are one of those people who does very well living in an area with a little bit of both.

Sometimes people who have too much yin Chi will prosper living in an area that has more yang Chi. The opposite also holds true. Where do you feel you would find the most harmony?

Assess where you live and ask yourself how your environment is making you feel? Is it Yin or Yang or balanced? What attracted you to the area? What changes in your life have occurred since you moved to this area? Are you more balanced?

Top Left: Dinosaur Provincial Park, Alberta
Middle Left: Bow River, Alberta
Bottom Left: Bonito, Brazil
Above: Managua, Nicaragua

Figure 5.1 The Bagua Map

Chapter 5.
Getting to Know Your Bagua Map

This simplified Feng Shui Bagua map reveals how the different areas of any space you occupy are connected to specific aspects of your life. Each section of the Bagua is a Chi Centre. Since space is a metaphor of your life, the Bagua can help you organize and improve your entire living area.

There are nine Chi Centres in your life. These include:

Prosperity/Wealth	Fame/Reputation	Relationships/Love
Family/Foundation	Health	Creativity/Children
Skills/Knowledge	Career/Life Path	Helpful People/Travel

The Bagua map provides us with the means to identify the key aspects of each Chi Centre and how to then balance these aspects to achieve ultimate happiness. If you pay attention to each of the Chi Centres, and make simple changes where needed, you can experience positive changes you had not thought possible.

Feng Shui can enhance any size of space, from stove tops to desk drawers to specific rooms to entire homes. Removing clutter allows new Chi to come into a space, which makes this one of the best ways to create quick, positive changes.

You can use all types of tools to ensure that Chi moves at a balanced pace around your home. These include the use of colour, sound, scent and movement and the elements of Water, Fire, Metal, Wood and Earth.

The Nine Chi Centres

The nine Chi Centres are like a road map of your space. By laying the grid over your floor plan the Centres that relate to each aspect of your life can be identified.

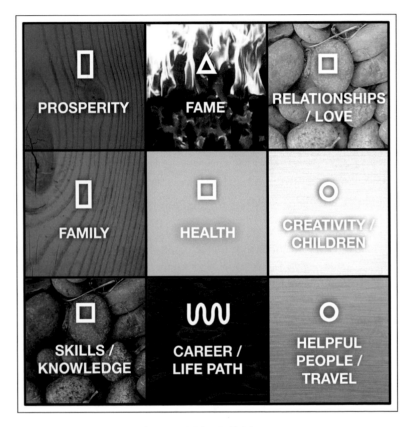

Figure 5.2 The 9 Chi Areas

To simplify the map, look at it like a grid of nine, positioned very much like a tick-tack-toe board.

When you superimpose the Bagua over your floor plan, it becomes a road map of your Chi forces, which you can then balance or enhance to bring you closer to your desired outcomes.

If you don't have your floor plan handy, I suggest you spend a few minutes drawing a rough layout of how the rooms are arranged in your home.

Laying Out Your Floor Plan

Divide your floor plan into nine equal Centres positioning the front door at the bottom. We always orientate the Bagua Map to the front door. This is the main entrance as designed by the architect and is referred to as the "Mouth of Chi" which is where the Chi physically enters your space. We would never orientate the map to the side door, back door or even the garage door entrance to the home.

The front door should fall within the Skills and Knowledge, Career and Life Path or Helpful People and Travel Chi Centres. Because there is no other place for the front door to be situated, the Bagua is precisely orientated to give an accurate reading.

Here is an example of the Bagua map superimposed over a main floor house plan (Figure 5.3). In this home, the front door falls in the Career and Life Path Chi Centre.

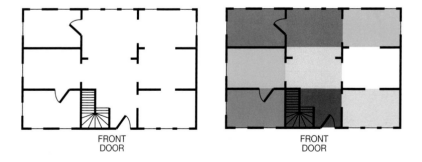

FRONT
DOOR

FRONT
DOOR

Figure 5.3 Laying Out Your Floor Plan

How Do You Lay Out Your Garage?

If your garage were distinctly separate from the main floor then you would treat it as though it were not part of your main living space. This is the case for the first two main floor layouts below.

In figure 5.4A, the garage does not impact the space. Here you would lay the Bagua on the main floor up to the inner walls of the garage and then lay the Bagua again for the garage itself.

In figure 5.4B, you would lay the Bagua on the main floor and then lay the Bagua again on the garage. The Bagua is rotated so the overhead garage door falls into the front three Chi Centres of Skills and Knowledge, Career and Life Path and Helpful People and Travel.

In figure 5.4C, the garage backs into the main floor of the house. In this case, you must treat the garage as part of the main floor.

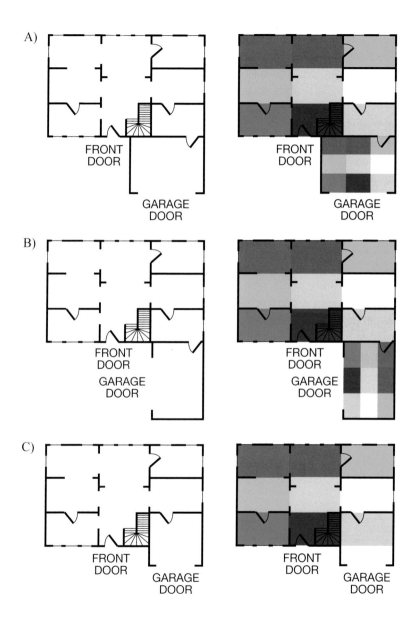

Figure 5.4 Laying Out Your Garage

Bonus and Missing Pieces

Not all homes are perfectly square or oblong like the house plans we have just studied (figure 5.5A). Some houses have pieces jutting out or jutting in. When laying the Bagua map, you will have to determine whether to include these jutting out or jutting in pieces. In Feng Shui, we clarify these pieces as either missing or bonus pieces. Missing pieces should be adjusted and filled in to allow more balance and harmony within the space.

In figure 5.5B, we are treating the jutting out section as a bonus piece. Note how all nine Chi Centres are intact and the bonus piece is being viewed as an extra area.

In figure 5.5C, we are including the jutting out section of the floor plan as an integral part of the Bagua. This means we are treating this plan as having a huge missing piece in the Relationships/Love and Creativity/Children Chi Centres.

Missing Or Bonus Pieces? How Will We Know?

First, we need to decide how much of the area is missing or impacting the floor space. Start by identifying and measuring the basic 4-wall construction of the floor plan, which is usually a rectangle or a square. If the habitable space protruding outside of the basic construction is more than 30% of the exterior wall measurement, in any one direction, it must be included into the floor plan. If it is less than 30%, it is considered a bonus energy area.

A second way of determining whether you have a bonus or missing piece is to assess what is happening in your life relating to that grid. Perhaps you have been losing money. In this case, chances are you are dealing with a missing piece in your Prosperity and Wealth Chi Centre. Here you will want to examine this area closely to see if anything needs to be added, repositioned or removed.

I once had a client whose floor plan had huge missing pieces in her Prosperity and Wealth and Relationships and Love Chi Centres. The consequences were devastating. Her relationship with her husband

A)

B)

C)

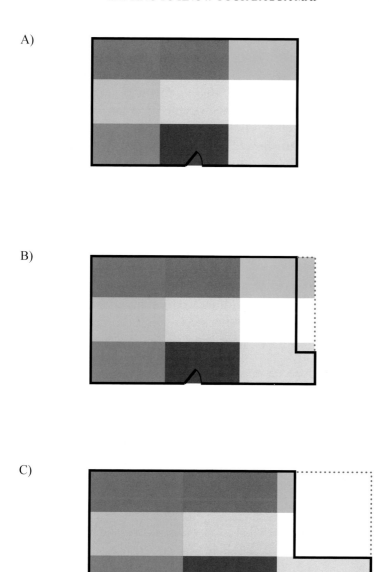

Figure 5.5 Bonus and Missing Pieces

of 17 years ended in divorce shortly after she moved in, and her Prosperity and Wealth was severely compromised by her situation.

What Can be Done to Fill in Missing Pieces?

When there are missing pieces, we can fill in the space where the walls would be. Expensive renovations are not necessary and can be simply achieved by using red tape, string, cord or even paint, so long as it is permanent and in the colour Red. The colour Red has a very powerful vibration of safety and security.

The lines you draw do not have to be visible; they can be buried in the ground. By filling in the missing piece you are energetically moving the wall so the square of the Bagua is completed. If this is not possible, you could plant a good-sized bush or tree exactly at the place where the two walls would meet if the piece were not missing. Or you could hang a crystal, mirror or use bright lights on the wall facing out to expand the missing piece.

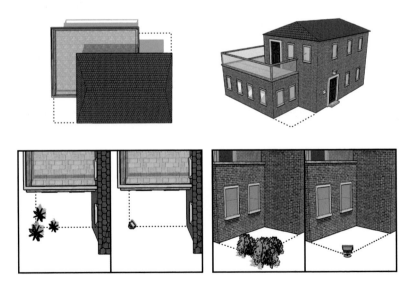

Figure 5.6 Bonus and Missing Pieces II

Chapter 6.
The Five Elements

The five elements are an important force behind Feng Shui. The interaction between them may be either positive or negative, depending on the relative balance each has on the other.

If you study the Bagua Map, you will see how each Chi Centre has an associated element, represented with a visual sign (Figure 6.1).

Balancing the elements is an important factor, and the Chinese believe that there is a great interplay of yin and yang. Difficulties are caused when one element dominants over the others. To reduce the negative effect, an opposite is applied.

When these five elements are in balance in your home, you will find that you have more balance in general. This means a better chance of getting what you want from life. You need your home to have the correct level of force so it can be working for you, rather than against you. It's a bit like a tug of war.

You can use the elements by placing them in the correct area of your home and giving intention that they work for your particular need. The fact that you have put your Chi into careful placement of these elements will start to cause the changes that can enhance your life.

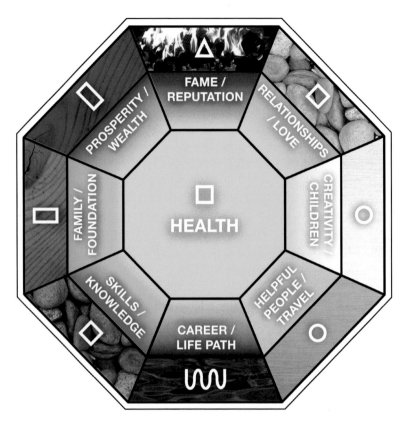

Triangle = Fire   Wavy Line = Water
Square = Earth   Rectangle = Wood
Circle = Metal

Figure 6.1 Symbols of the Five Elements

Fire

Fire is an upward Chi, which has hot explosive fiery Chi. This is a great element to use when you are looking for change because it is bright, clear, and a good Chi attracter. As Fire is red, its associated colour is Red and its corresponding geometric shape is a triangle or pyramid. Its natural position is in the Fame and Reputation Chi Centre of the Bagua, but it can also be used to bring change to any area. If your career needs a little boosting, I suggest placing something from this Chi force to stimulate the desire.

This element is also associated with the heart and therefore brings warmth and passion. However, Fire is extremely powerful and can destroy and explode into aggression if the force is not in balance.

A fireplace or candles positioned in this area are wonderful ways of using this force. Candles and fireplaces do not have to be lit to be effective. It is the Fire they represent that's important. Other ways of using this force are to add bright lights, lamps, or items made from fur, leather or wool.

Artwork is an excellent way of depicting the elements; pictures of animals are a perfect addition. Animals have a wonderful fiery force about them, and, in Feng Shui, animals are referred to as having hot, explosive Chi.

Famous people or people of great strength are a terrific adaptation of Fire forces. People you admire and look up to have a strong, inspirational Chi. Pictures of mountains, which are solid and of great force, are ideal. You might also add pictures of sunrises and sunsets or perhaps even a volcano erupting fire.

Earth

The Earth element has a stabilizing Chi to it, which balances and grounds us. When life becomes quite intense, Earth helps us become more centred and connected. This element is located in the Health, Relationships and Love and Skills and Knowledge Chi Centres. The colours for this element include yellow and earth tones.

Earth is associated with the stomach and its shape is square. Balancing this element enhances control and alleviates fear in your life and allows the natural progression of life to unfold. Too much of this element causes the natural flow to be blocked.

There is much you can do to bring the Earth element into your home. When my girls were young they could be quite excitable at bedtime and would have difficulty settling down in their rooms. I found four smooth rocks, each the size of a baseball, and placed them in the four corners of their room. This calmed the Chi down and helped the girls to feel more grounded and settled for a good night's sleep. I even let them paint the rocks!

Rocks are not the only way to add this element. Other additions include ceramics or earthenware, brick or tile, pebbles, natural crystals, gemstones, marble or granite. Artwork of landscapes, fields and mountains can have the same grounding influence.

Metal

Metal is a cold, dense Chi. It is associated with communication, creativity, detail, symbols, signals and noise. The colour of this element is white and its shape is a circle, sphere and dome. Metal is associated with the mouth and lungs and is located in Creativity and Children, and Helpful People and Travel Chi Centres.

This element is used when you want to improve communications, empower your children, or stimulate your projects. To enhance one's voice, to speak with clarity and authority. However, overly used and it has the Chi of a sharp knife and can severely affect your nervous disposition and your level of alertness and focus.

All types of metals are associated with this element, including stainless steel, copper, brass and iron, silver and gold.

I have enhanced these elements into my home by adding a metal toy train into my Helpful People & Travel and into my Creativity & Children I have placed my telephone here to aid good communications.

To enhance the Metal Element, add artwork depicting man-made structures like buildings or bridges.

Water

Water has the Chi of stillness. Water is the Chi of things moving downward and coming to rest. It is deep, thoughtful, fluid, reflective and still. The colours for this element are black and dark blue. Water, which is associated with the kidneys, has a natural position in the Career and Life Path Chi Centres and has the ability to increase the flow of people to you and bring cash into your life.

The shape for this element is a wavy, undulating, free form that appears to fill space just like water does. A leakage of this element can have a draining affect in your life and you will feel the emotion of depression and stress not to mention a loss in your finances. Too much of this element has a drowning effect on your life and the positive Chi will have a soggy effect and slow down your career and life progress.

I have a beautiful water fountain on my driveway, which is so peaceful and relaxing to listen to and watch. As I live in Canada, during the winter months the fountain must stay empty. This does not affect the power of the fountain because, symbolically, it still attracts this Chi to my home.

Other ways of using this element include the addition of streams, pools and any type of water feature. Even a dry riverbed works well for what it symbolizes. Feng Shui crystals, glass and mirrors are also helpful, as is artwork of lakes, rivers, oceans, waterfalls and snow.

To help bring the Water Element into my home, I have pictures of fishing boats. Remember, if you choose sailing pictures the sails need to be pointing towards the home and not out the door. Otherwise, this represents money leaving the home.

Wood

This element is associated with expansion and new growth. It's climbing Chi encourages progress and advancement into one's life. Over use of this element can cause obesity and a tendency of laziness with a lowered immune system to be prone to colds and flu.

The colour is green and is related to the liver. Wood's shape is a column or rectangle positioned upright, like a skyscraper.

This element is well situated in the Family and Foundation and Prosperity and Wealth Chi Centres. It has an expansive, growing, flexible, and tough, upward Chi. You will find the Wood element in healthy thriving plants or silk plants, wooden furniture, wood paneling, and natural fibres like cotton and silk. Fabrics, wallpaper and curtains with a floral print work well here.

You could also add artwork with forests, gardens and flowers.

I painted my daughter's room in a warm shade of green. Green is a growth Chi that helped her to evolve as she matured from a child into a young woman.

Ensuring The Elements Work Together In Our Home
As well as placing the element in the appropriate space in your home, you can use the other elements to help enhance or reduce the effect of a particular element.

Perhaps you have a Chi Centre that is Wood, (such as the Family and Foundation Chi Centre), but you do not want to introduce more Wood into that area. Instead, you could add one of the other elements that actually builds on the Wood elements that are currently there.

The Building Cycle
When elements work together, we call this the building cycle. Here's how the building cycle is described: Water feeds Wood; Wood fuels Fire; Fire makes Earth; Earth creates Metal; and Metal creates Water.

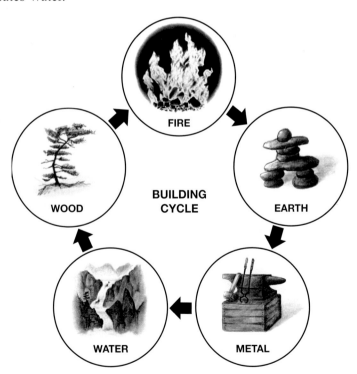

Figure 6.2 The Building Cycle

How Metal creates Water is the most difficult concept to grasp. Think of it this way. If you take a metal object like a bowl and leave it out overnight, you will find condensation (or water) on the bowl by morning.

Here's an example of where you might use the building cycle. Let's say you want to improve your reputation and in the Fame and Reputation Chi Centre you currently have candles and triangular-shaped objects. If you don't want to add more Fire elements, you can add Wood instead - even something as simple as a wooden-framed picture - which works to build Fire. Adding the colour green, which is the colour associated with Wood, will also help build Fire.

The Reducing Cycle
Sometimes we don't want to build more of an element within a Chi Centre, we want to reduce its force instead. We call this a reducing cycle. Here's how it works: Water douses Fire; Fire melts Metal; Metal chops Wood; Wood penetrates Earth; and Earth dams Water.

Let's say you have a room in the Prosperity and Wealth Chi Centre, which is a Wood Chi Centre. This room is dominantly white - the walls, the carpet, the window frames - and you want to keep it that way. The predominance of white makes the room very Metal. As Metal chops Wood, all this Metal Chi is negatively impacting the natural Wood element's regard for prosperity.

To bring this room back into balance, we would need to reduce the influence of Metal by adding the element of Fire. (Remember, Fire melts Metal.) We could add candles, the colour red or triangular objects. If these items don't fit with your décor, they can be hidden. Whether they are visible or not, they still bring a powerful balancing effect. You might want to add a red sticky dot or paper behind pictures or under the sofa or use liner paper inside drawers. Be creative with your thinking.

Elements can be represented in a room even if you cannot see them.
Placing an element behind an object still brings a powerful balancing
effect. If you drop something down the side of the sofa that should
not be there, say potato chips or your kids' favourite gum, the Chi
vibration of those items will reflect and cause a shift in the Chi.
Everything has Chi. You want to be sure the Chi works positively, in
ways that you intend.

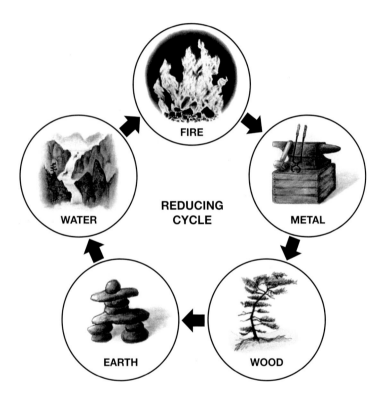

Figure 6.3 The Reducing Cycle

Chapter 7.
A Look at Each of the Bagua Chi Centres

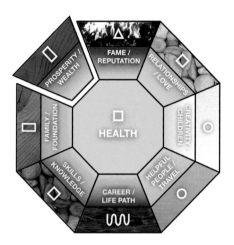

Prosperity and Wealth Chi Centre

The Prosperity and Wealth Chi Centre is located in the back upper-left section of the Bagua and relates to your good fortune, your monetary estate and your possessions. This area is connected with your cash flow, your financial situation and your flow of finances. Cash is not the only abundance in your life. Prosperity and Wealth Chi relates to all those things you wish abundance of - including health, wealth and happiness.

This Chi Centre should not be used as a storage space.

Since many people want to increase their abundance of cash, this area is probably one of the most popular reasons people will seek advice from Feng Shui. If you, too, need to earn more or wish to increase the flow of this Chi, then the Prosperity and Wealth Centre will be an area to focus your attention on.

One way to fuel the Chi associated with abundance is to add the colours of purple, green and red. These colours have a rich Chi vibration and are a wonderful way of stimulating the Chi. You can add these colours in many ways, without necessarily changing the colour of your walls!

Prosperity and Wealth Chi Centre

+ Force Builders	- Force Reducers
Wood Element, healthy plants or silks	Metal Element: stainless steel, copper, brass and silver
Colours: purple, green, red and gold items	Colours white or grey
Columnar Shape objects	Circle shaped objects
Building Cycle Element: Water	Bathrooms
Money or Valuables such as jewellery	Storage
Chinese money	Clutter

In addition to balancing the Wood Element consider adding symbolic items that represents abundance. One of my students used coins to stimulate the Chi associated with bringing money in. Maybe you could put some coins in a wooden goblet.

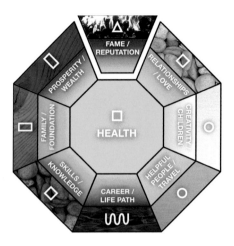

Fame and Reputation Chi Centre

The Fame and Reputation Chi Centre represents your fame and reputation and how others perceive you. It relates to your popularity in the workplace and in social activities like team sports and other involvements within your community.

Fame and Reputation is a Fire Chi Centre. A reputation that has been earned by honesty inspires greatness and fuels the flame of fame. Conversely, a bad reputation will stick with you for a very long time.

You can elevate your enthusiasm, passion for life and inspiration by adding the colour red to this Chi Centre. This is especially important if you are setting new goals or putting a plan in place for your future. Ensure you are clear about what you are elevating, or you may be recognised for more than you wished for.

Adding items in a triangular shape can simply be added to symbolically represent this Chi of Fire. A pyramid shape Crystal Lamp works wonders in my home or simply placing artwork of animals or exhibit your family pet portrait in this location raises the Chi significantly. Animals are referred to having hot explosive fire Chi in Feng Shui.

Fame and Reputation Chi Centre

+ Force Builders	- Force Reducers
Fire Element: fireplace, candles, lamps, lights, fur or leather	Water
Colour: Red	Colours: Black or dark blue
Triangular shaped objects	Wavy line shaped objects
Building Cycle Element: Wood	Bathrooms
Awards or certificates of achievements	Mirrors
Artwork or ornaments of animals, the sun, volcanoes or fireworks, healthy plants	Negative items relating to negativity in any way

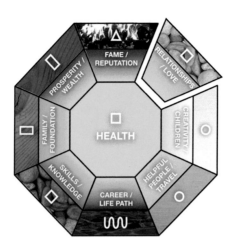

Relationships and Love Chi Centre

The Relationships and Love Chi Centre specifically relates to the status of your existing relationship with your partner or your ability to find a new partner in either your personal or business life.

Relationships and Love Chi Centre

+ Force Builders	- Force Reducers
Earth Element: Ceramics, earthenware, brick, rock, natural crystal, gemstones	Wood Element
Colours: Pink, red and white	Colours: green and blue
Square shaped objects, candlesticks, books and romantic figurines	Columnar, rectangle shaped objects
Mementos from your romantic experiences with your present partner	Twin beds
Artwork depicting romance and love	Mirrors in bedrooms
Poetry or quotes and sayings about love and romance	Belongings from a negative past or relationship

In order to find meaningful relationships with others, we must first start by truly loving ourselves. Only when we are open and loving to our own needs, wishes and aspirations, can we open our hearts to others. By loving yourself, you enhance your own personal Chi. This is precisely what attracts others to loving you too.

To achieve self-love you must learn to treat yourself with respect and now is an ideal time to become more generous and self-forgiving. Make an affirmation to be more positive.

Say to yourself: "I am using the Force behind Feng Shui for the better. Change brings magnificent renewal into my life. I embrace change, and change lovingly embraces me."

This area is the only Chi Centre where you would put things in pairs. Try to position everything in sets of two, including candlesticks, night tables and bedside lamps.

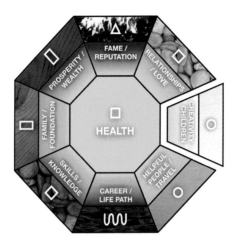

Creativity and Children Chi Centre

The Creativity and Children Chi Centre is associated with your creative side. It relates to projects you are working on and the quality of communication with your children or co-workers.

We are all creators in our lives. We create new cells in our body all the time; our minds are always creating new ideas. Creativity and time with children help provide joy and encouragement.

The key to attaining our full creative potential is to be joyous while participating in creative activities. If we enjoy the process, the creative mind explodes with new ideas.

When we watch children using their creative skills we see an abundance of joy. It is the pure childlike quality of joy within us all that carries the creative spirit.

To stimulate your creativity, bring into this Chi Centre art or objects that are particularly creative, playful and colourful. Adding the colour white and the element Metal will help to improve the quality of your communication.

If the space permits, add toys, dolls and stuffed animals that bring you joy, as well as photographs of your children, grandchildren or any child - preferably in metal frames. Pictures that children have made are wonderful to display in this Chi Centre. I have a beautiful picture of my daughter's hand that she created when still in kindergarten.

Also, pictures or objects of man-made structures like bridges or architecture are a wonderful way of stimulating the Chi here.

Creativity and Children Chi Centre

+ Force Builders	- Force Reducers
Metal Element: stainless steel, copper, brass or silver	Fire Element
Colour: white	Colour: red
Circle or sphere shape	Triangular shaped objects
Electrical equipment, entertainment centres	Negative representations from literature
Soft toys or animals, games, children's artwork, baby pictures or photographs of children	Alcohol
	Weapons
Hobby supplies	

Helpful People And Travel Chi Centre

The Helpful People and Travel Chi Centre is about attracting helpful people into your life and relying on their support. If you find you get taken for granted, or sometimes feel you wear a "kick me" sign on your back, this Centre deserves extra attention.

Likewise, you might want to attract more people who you believe can help you achieve a specific goal. So many people can be helpful in your life: mentors, clients, customers, employees or colleagues.

Your safe travels are connected in this Chi Centre. Maybe you wish to travel more, take more family vacations to exotic places or perhaps you travel more than you wish too.

This Chi Centre should not be used as a storage space.

Helpful People and Travel is a spiritual Chi Centre. This is an excellent place to display pictures of Buddha, your guardian angels or even your little talismans. These would be seen as the "Ultimate Helpful People" to provide spiritual guidance in your life.

Here you can also place a metal container holding your wishes. You might want to write the names of three people you believe can help you achieve your goals, or find pictures of three items you hope for (e.g., a new car, new dining table and a diamond ring.) Add your travel brochures here for that dream vacation. This worked for me! I went on a dream cruise with my family after placing the brochure in my wish container.

Add the colours grey, white and black to this Chi Centre together with the element Metal. You could display pictures of man-made structures like cars, buildings, ships or bridges in metal frames. I have even put a train set here, which I inherited from my father. It works perfectly.

Helpful People and Travel Chi Centre

+ **Force Builders**	- **Force Reducers**
Metal Element: stainless steel, copper, brass or silver	Fire Element
Colours: grey, white and black	Colour: Red
Circle or sphere shape	Triangular shaped objects
Inspiring artwork relating to travel, like planes, trains and automobiles	Storage
Bridges or architecture made of metal	Garbage
Spiritual items like your talismans or guardian angels that represent the ultimate helpful people in your life	

Career and Life Path Chi Centre

The Career and Life-path Chi Centre represents your work, career success and how you earn your money. It also represents where your life is going.

You might be looking for a change in life direction such as a job change, a new volunteer role in your community or a switch to a different vocation.

Add the colours black and dark blue, and the element Water to make changes in this Chi Centre.

You might want to add a fish tank here, or pictures of boats or ships. Be sure that they are pointing towards your home. Sailing away can work against you by symbolizing your abundance flowing away. Keep the Chi flowing towards you with the vessel sailing into your home.

Mirrors and glass objects act like water too: they are reflective and fluid. They are particularly advantageous when placed by the front door, it reflects the Chi into the home. Ensure that the mirror is not facing the front door otherwise your Chi will be reflected straight back out.

You can place a water feature here, too, either on the inside or outside of the front door, depending on your weather. This symbolizes movement and the attraction of opportunities into your life. Hanging a metal wind-chime shifts negative Chi and stimulates changes in your life. Ensure that the sound quality is of a high standard and loved by all who occupy the space.

Career and Life Path Chi Centre

+ **Force Builders**	- **Force Reducers**
Water Element: fountains and fish tanks	Earth Element
Colours: black and dark blue	Colours: green and pink
Wavy line shape	Square shaped objects
Glass	Artwork depicting mountains and landscapes
Mirrors	Earthenware, pottery or ceramics
Artwork containing water, ships or boats sailing into the home	

Skills and Knowledge Chi Centre
The Skills and Knowledge Chi Centre involves your ability to learn, make wise decisions and improve yourself. In other words, to become smarter, wiser or wittier!

Skills and Knowledge is a spiritual Chi Centre and is associated with your spiritual or religious life and self-development.

Display your mystical advisers or gurus to help develop your teachings.

You may be having a hard time at work or feel you lack wisdom or the ability to make good decisions. Perhaps you would like to change your career, but you question your skills and ability to move into a new area.

Add the colours blue, green and black and the element Earth to this Chi Centre. Ensure that the colours are uplifting and are not of a darkened shade which will cloud your judgement and clarity of thought.

To stimulate success, add photographs or certificates of your achievements here. Inspirational words with those lovely pictures are a perfect addition. I recently bought a lighthouse picture for my daughter with the words, "The secret of success in life is to be ready for opportunity when it comes." Filling your library with inspirational books that nurtures the mind also increases the Chi here.

Skills and Knowledge Chi Centre

+ **Force Builders**	- **Force Reducers**
Earth Element: Ceramics, earthenware, brick, rock, natural crystal, gemstones Colours: blue, green and black	Wood Element Colours: Dark green and dark blue
Square shape	Rectangle or columnar shapes
Inspirational books, CDs and DVDs	Artwork of trees, flowers or forests
Artwork with inspiring words or photographs of people who inspire and educate you	
Spiritual symbols	

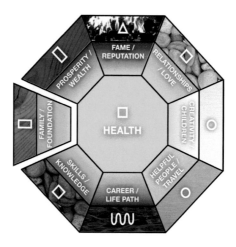

Family and Foundation

The Family and Foundation Chi Centre represents all your family members including parents as well as those close to you such as friends, your superiors and authority figures. It involves family dynamics and interactions. Maybe you are not part of the family bloodline and wish to feel more included, or perhaps you are a family that is blended, bringing two families together.

Starting a family can also be achieved here as you improve the energy and clear away blockages that may prevent fresh Chi from entering your space.

This would be an area to focus on to promote harmony at home or work, or at social clubs or organizations where you work together as a team.

Family and Foundation Chi Centre

+ Force Builders	- Force Builders
Wood Element: Fresh flowers, plants or wooden furniture	Metal Element
Colours: green and blue	Colours: white or grey
Rectangle or columnar shape	Circle or sphere shaped objects
Family, friends or team photographs	Weapons
Artwork with plants, flowers or trees	Negative items from family, friends or teams
Family heirlooms	

In business, working on this area can improve relationships with employees and peers. Enhancing the Chi will help create a positive working environment and happy employees.

Add the colours green and blue and the element Wood. This is also a great place to hang your family portraits, team pictures or wedding photographs.

Health Chi Centre

The most important Health Chi Centre promotes balance and can directly affect your physical and mental health.

Once you have balanced all the Chi Centres you will naturally bring into harmony the Health Centre. However, this is one Centre that does not want to be missed, and you should ensure that nothing blocks the Chi here.

This Chi Centre should not be used as a storage space. The Chi needs to flow in an open manner.

Also check to see if your staircase is located within your Health Chi Centre. This can create chaotic, downward-spiralling Chi and can cause issues with your mental and physical health. I had a client whose staircase was in her Health Centre and she fell down the stairs and broke her back! This had a tremendous negative effect on her, both mentally and physically. When staircases fall in the Health area, I recommend adding a crystal in the centre of the ceiling above the staircase to redirect the Chi.

Ask yourself honestly about your current state of health, whether mental or physical. What about other members in your household? Do you find that you or family members are always catching the latest strain of flu or colds? Do you often feel down or depressed?

You can enhance the Chi in this area with yellow and earth tone colours combined with the element Earth. This will improve your vitality and stamina and help you feel more in control of your life.

Health Chi Centre

+ **Force Builders**	- **Force Reducers**
Earth Element: Ceramics, earthenware, brick, rock, natural crystal, gemstones	Wood Element
Colours: yellow and earth tone	Colours: Green, blue, pink or red
Square shaped objects	Wooden objects
Symbolic items relating to health, peace and tranquility	Storage
Fresh fruit, vegetables or yellow flowers	Staircases
Artwork depicting the earth	Bathrooms
	Stoves

Maintain Balance

If your Chi Centres are not in balance then you can unknowingly cause unevenness between areas. To illustrate this point, think about how many people struggle to achieve work-life balance. They work hard on their careers, only to find their relationships suffer. Too

many hours at the office and not enough time at home translates to STRESS. We feel guilty for not spending enough time with our loved ones, but at the same time we feel the pressure to provide financially for them.

If you feel there is a place in your home - or your life - that seems out of balance, then you can use Feng Shui to modify the flow of Chi. Use the Five Elements to enhance or reduce each Chi Centre.

Chapter 8.
Giving Power to Feng Shui with Intentions and Goal Setting

An intention is deciding what you want to achieve when you make Feng Shui changes within your surroundings. It is through our intentions that we give power to Feng Shui changes. The physical cure is said to influence the Chi by about 30%, the remaining 70% is influenced by your intention when applying the cure.

If you want to improve a certain aspect in your life, you would need to locate the appropriate Chi Centre. By tuning into the Chi, you can better determine what may be blocking the Chi from moving fluidly and thus preventing you from achieving what you want. For example, let's say you are having difficulty feeling close to your partner. This means that more attention is needed in the Relationships and Love Chi Centre. Make your physical changes and reinforce with intentions.

Your intention can be set through writing goals and using prayer, meditation, visualization or affirmation.

It is very important to refine your intentions for each of the Chi Centres. If you are not clear about what you want, how can you expect Feng Shui to deliver on your intentions?

You likely have many examples from your life when your intentions were unclear to either you or others. Think of past birthdays. How many times did you know exactly what presents you wanted, yet for some reason you forgot to convey your ideas to friends and family? Without access to your wish list, your loved ones bought you something you didn't really want, and you ended up feeling disappointed.

Once your intention has been made, it's important to set a specific goal related to that intention. You would not set out on a long car journey without a map and directions. Chi is like that, too.

Setting goals will help you to create a feeling of possibility and focus on where you want to go with your life. Be sure to be specific about what you want. Use your five senses: sight, touch, smell, sound and taste. Write down your goal and read it back to yourself every day, visualizing your life as if that goal is already obtained.

Here are a few examples of how intentions have worked in my life.

Purchasing a New Car with Intention
When I made an intention that I wanted a new car, I set a specific goal to make it happen. First, I decided on the car I wanted. Then, I set about doing my research, which included a trip to the show room and a test drive on the open road.

Throughout this process, I tried to consciously engage all of my senses. I made a mental picture of the outside and inside details of the car. When I sat in the car I felt the steering wheel and noticed the smell of the leather and even the taste of that smell. I listened to the sound of the engine and the stereo sound system.

Before I left the show room I picked up a glossy brochure, which detailed all the car's features. When I got home, I placed the brochure in my Helpful People and Travel Chi Centre to be a constant reminder of my goal.

Each day, I would sit and visualise my new car as if it was already mine. I would picture the car sitting in my garage. Then I would see myself opening the car door, climbing into the driver's seat, fastening my seat belt, and turning the key in the ignition. I would remember the smell of the new leather, the taste in my mouth, and the sound of the engine as I turned the key.

After visualizing my new car, I simply let it go, releasing my intention to the universe. Intentions - backed with specific goals - are powerful forces. Using all your senses to visualize your goal creates an extra boost. Six weeks after my first trip to the show room, I was back again to pick up my new car.

Immigrating to Canada

In 1999, I lived in a small village just outside of Weston Super Mare, Somerset in England. I was very happy, living a life full of joy with my husband, John, and our three small children. But as time went by, John and I were becoming increasingly restless, yearning to explore new lands beyond England.

The Hankins Family

John was busy completing his MBA at Bath University, while also holding down a good position that required extensive world travel. It sounds exciting, but as a family man, his heart wanted to be with our small children and me.

We were also rapidly outgrowing our space. Homes in England are small and prices high. After evaluating the market, we decided our best option was to add a conservatory (sun room) to give us more living space. When John returned from a September visit to the Far East, I proudly presented him with an abundance of research for various conservatories, feeling sure he would be impressed by my efforts. His response was not at all what I expected. He did not even look at the brochures and posed this question instead: "Should we look to emigrate to Canada?" I simply whisked the brochures into the waste paper basket and excitedly answered, "Yes".

I have never been a scholar nor, for that matter, a big reader. I didn't even know where the library was. But this was my research challenge and I eagerly set out. The helpful librarian took me to the relevant reference book, which fell open to a page that advertised 'Canada News'. It gave everything we needed to test our eligibility for moving to Canada. At that time, the target number was 70. When I did the calculations, I found we had that magic number.

We decided to bite the bullet and go for it. We submitted our application to the Canadian Embassy in London on December 4th, 1999. While we'd heard that the application process could take up to two years, we received notification over Christmas that we had been issued a file number.

The next question was where to settle. We had previously vacationed in Vancouver and had fallen in love with the space, beauty and friendly people. But given all the Calgary success stories shared in Canada News, we thought we should at least take a look at this city, despite the tales we'd heard about their cold winters. In February we headed to Calgary for a two-week fact finding mission. When John and I arrived, there was not a single snowflake on the ground. The next morning, we awoke to 20 centimetres of snow! We were totally amazed and excited. Neither of us had seen snow like this before.

The trip was wonderful. On our last day, as we sat supping our hot coffee and tucking into a lovely donut at Tim Horton's, John turned to me and asked, "Do you think we could live here?" My reply: "Absolutely".

Three days after our return to England, we received a lovely letter from the Canadian High Commission advising us that our application had been accepted subject to a positive health check. We were amazed that this would happen so quickly. While we were completing the health requirements, we enlisted an estate agent (realtor) to evaluate our home. She was so enthralled that she lined up three possible buyers within a few days. This put us in a rather difficult position. We had not actually received our visas at this point, and it would mean that we would be homeless. But as so often happens, the Feng Shui took care of this too. On April 11th, 2000, just three weeks later, a parcel arrived with our visas to Canada.

Here we were, seven months from the point of considering emigrating, to having our visas in our hands!

On July 8th, 2000, we flew to Calgary, our new home, with our three girls in tow. We've since moved to an acreage by Okotoks, which is just south of the city. We now live in our dream home, a space where we can be one with nature and enjoy a panoramic view of the mountains. It was here that I felt compelled to Feng Shui our garden. While I had always been attracted to the strange forces of Chi, I'd not yet received formal training. Yet again, the universe provided. What do I find in my mailbox but a local college catalogue advertising Feng Shui classes! I could not believe my luck. And I've been pursuing my dreams ever since.

Intentions

+	-
Force Builders	**Force Reducers**
Being clear	Being vague
Committing intentions to paper	Procrastinating
Visualizing	Having no faith

Chapter 9.
Introduction to Cures

What I love about Feng Shui is that there is always a cure. By "cure" we simply mean a Feng Shui solution, one that involves an action that redirects Chi flow to create a positive change. No matter what your situation, you can find ways around it without having to resort to expensive renovations such as knocking down walls or moving lock, stock and barrel.

I've seen so many Feng Shui success stories with clients and students. Just recently, for example, I received a call from a wonderful couple trying desperately to sell their home. They were on a tight deadline to relocate to another country, and despite a buoyant real estate market and a beautiful home in a great location, their house would not budge. During my initial consultation, I found nothing immediately to pinpoint their specific dilemma. We were chatting over a cup of tea when the topic of dead Chi came up. I explained how dried flowers and potpourri could actually stagnate the Chi. At this point the gentleman folded his arms, threw back his head with a huge bellow of laughter and said, "I don't suppose it helps to have your dead mother's ashes in your desk drawer."

As it happened, the drawer in question was located in their Career and Life Path Chi Centre, the very place that manifests a change in life direction. The couple readily agreed to have the ashes removed by day's end, which was something they'd been thinking of doing, but hadn't made a priority. That evening they released his mother's ashes to a beautiful flowing river, sending their love with her. When they returned home, they placed the urn in the garbage bin located in their garage. A few days passed before the garbage collectors came by. As the couple watched the truck drive down the street the telephone rang with a call from their realtor. They had three viewings set up for that afternoon and they successfully sold their home that very evening.

Cures can work for even the most sceptical. A friend of mine had been trying to sell her house for nearly 18 months when she reluctantly called for some Feng Shui advice. She certainly wasn't convinced about the notion of balancing Chi and enticing the Chi into her home, but by this point she felt she had nothing to lose. Her home was well priced, tastefully decorated and nestled within a friendly neighbourhood. So why wasn't it selling? I felt the problem might be the home's positioning in the corner of the cul-de-sac, which was making it difficult for the Chi to move. Imagine a gentle stream meandering along the street and then spilling out into a pool that has no exit. The water becomes stagnant and dead. This is the same effect it has on Chi.

I recommended my friend purchase a water fountain for her front yard and add some lighting along the footpath to guide the Chi to her front door. She called me six weeks later with the exciting news. She confessed that she was not convinced that this would work and had procrastinated for weeks. When she finally decided enough was enough, she went out and purchased a beautiful, inexpensive water fountain for her front garden. After she set up her new fountain, it was a matter of mere days before her house sold.

Feng Shui cures can even help guide new life into this world. One of my students hesitantly approached me at the end of a class and asked if there was anything that Feng Shui could do to help her daughter conceive a baby. Her daughter had been trying unsuccessfully to get pregnant for several years, investing a great deal of time and money for in vitro fertilization treatments.

I suggested her daughter might want to spend time in her Creativity and Children Chi Centre, adding pictures or mementos of children and paying careful attention to clearing away all clutter. I also suggested that she plant a tree in the garden, ideally a tree that bears fruit, as this represents the reproduction of life. Once planted, she could pour her intention into nurturing and caring for the tree as though it was a child.

My student was practically glowing when she attended another class a few months later. She was excitedly anticipating the pending birth of her grandchild.

The Categories of Basic Cures
Basic cures in Feng Shui are divided into categories that include light, sound, living things, colour, water, moving objects, weight and fragrance. In each case, these cures are used to generate, anchor, deflect or absorb Chi.

In this chapter, we're going to look at the basic cures that will help to modify the flow of Chi in your home. Remember, intention is a crucial part of the process. Be sure to keep your intention at the forefront of your thoughts while choosing the physical cures you want to apply.

Light
The use of light is a great way of lifting the Chi in any particularly dull, dark or yin area of your home. Light brings new energizing life to an area by adding yang Chi. Imagine how your Chi feels in a dark room. There's a good chance you feel insecure, unnerved or passive. Now imagine adding light - yang Chi. You instantly change your Chi level by bringing security to the room.

With the use of light we can also reflect Chi that is flowing away from the home. Homes with walkout basements need this particular help because the land is sloping downwards and the Chi flows away. We can reflect this Chi back by shining light towards the home.

Light surrounding your home can be used strategically to give you positive results. In Feng Shui, the front of your lot represents the past, the middle the present, and the back the future. There is no better way to enhance the Chi in your lot than by placing lights along the back of your boundary fence, as this promotes your future.

Crystals

Feng Shui crystals are another powerful way of attracting Chi and bringing balance to an area. Crystals add light, which expands the area with new Chi. Because crystals are spheres, they redirect Chi and bring balance to chaotic Chi. Crystals also protect against poison arrows by reflecting and diffusing negative Chi flows. Poison arrows, also known as 'Sha Chi' or 'Secret Arrows' are sharp, fast moving Chi, usually caused by sharp corners or edges from furniture, columns or overhead beams.

When buying crystals for a Feng Shui cure, choose a round faceted shape and hang on nine (or multiples of nine) inches or centimetres of red ribbon or cord. Nine is considered the number of complete balance. A Feng Shui Crystal has a minimum of thirty two percent lead, which is optically pure, providing a spectacular light refraction.

Crystals can also be placed in a purse, backpack or briefcase. This ensures a good flow of Chi where ever you go. I suggest you carry a 20mm crystal to promote protection of your personal Chi.

To slow down the flow of Chi leaving your space, you can hang 30mm crystals wherever an exterior door leaves the home. A door in a bedroom leading to a patio or garden represents one partner leaving the relationship. One of my clients found herself in this situation. She had a door leading to a balcony and she couldn't understand why she could not keep a lasting relationship.

I suggest using 40 mm crystals where the area is large or the problem is quite serious. If your front door and back door align, for example, or when the stairs face the front door, Chi tends to rush out the door. In these cases, a 40 mm crystal is helpful.

To further balance the Chi of a room, add 30mm crystals to:

- Ceiling fans, which cause a tremendous amount of funnelling, chaotic Chi
- Rooms that do not have windows. The crystal expands the light and therefore increases the Chi
- The front of bedroom doors that leads to the outside
- Your home office, positioned directly above your office chair to promote clarity of thought
- Above the microwave oven to redirect negative electrical-magnetic frequency (EMF) emissions. The crystal can be placed in a cupboard if you do not wish it to be seen

As a general rule, clear crystals are used. Colour crystals, however, can promote the right types of Chi in each of the Chi Centres. Here's how colour can be incorporated:

Red - Red is used to stimulate the Chi through the vibration of its colour. Hang a red crystal in any Chi Centre that needs a kick-start. For example, red crystals hung from the centre of the bedroom ceiling help inspire love and passion. These crystals can also be used as colour cures in the Prosperity and Wealth, Fame and Reputation or Relationships and Love Chi Centres.

Purple - Purple vibrates with the Chi of nobility. This Chi has characteristics that encourage success in life, assist with self-esteem and attract great abundance. Purple works best in the Prosperity and Wealth Chi Centre and equally well for the money Chi Centres, which include the front door and stove.

Pink - Pink stimulates Love Chi and can be used as a colour cure in the Relationships and Love Chi Centre. You can hang a pink crystal from the master bedroom ceiling.

Green - Green is used in the Family and Foundation Chi Centre to promote the Chi to improve family relationships. Green is the colour of Wood Chi and has expansive, growing and upward moving characteristics. Green can also be used as a colour cure in the Family and Foundation, Skills and Knowledge, and Prosperity and Wealth Chi Centres.

Yellow - Yellow vibrates with the Chi of balance. This Chi has characteristics that promote improvement in both mental and physical health. Yellow crystals make an excellent Health Chi Centre cure and can also be used in any Chi Centre that needs additional balancing.

Blue - Blue vibrates with the spiritual Chi and the Chi of hope. This colour promotes calm and stillness. Improve your personal spiritual growth by hanging blue crystals in either of the spiritual Chi Centres - Skills and Knowledge or Helpful People and Travel. This is also a good colour for the Family and Foundation Chi Centre. Blue helps provide a calming Chi to any Chi Centre in your home if it is undergoing upheaval.

Sound
Have you noticed what happens to the Chi of a room when you turn on the radio? Sound is a wonderful way of elevating your Chi frequency. What do you feel when you hear a peel of church bells or a quiet piano melody? What about heavy rock music? Think about which sounds you find pleasant or unpleasant and how they affect you physically and emotionally.

Bells and wind chimes create wonderful sound that raise the Chi frequency and attract change in the Chi. Bamboo flutes, in particular, have special characteristics. The Chinese believe that when one lives with bamboo, one's life will improve in stages over time. A bamboo flute drives away negative Chi by communicating peace and safety through the sound it emits.

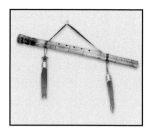

When buying a flute, you should look for the kind of bamboo in which each section grows longer than the previous one. This symbolizes life climbing upward step by step, meaning that things will get better for you tomorrow than they are today, even better the day after, and so on.

The ridges, which are the round circles on the bamboo, are very important in their Chi vibration. Try to purchase a bamboo flute that has the ridges intact. When the ridges are sanded off so they are smooth and unsegmented, the flute becomes much weaker. Hang the flutes with the shorter segments lower and the longer segments higher.

Ensure that your bamboo flute is treated with the greatest of respect; it should never be played with, handled roughly, or blown into. If this happens, the flute becomes simply an object of décor rather than an energetic cure.

As with crystals, your bamboo flute should be hung with red ribbon with two red tassels, one connected to each point where the ribbon attaches to the flute. Again, hang in multiples of nine inches, which represents the number of complete balance.

In Feng Shui, beams within a home are thought to shoot out poison arrows. Flutes can be used to cure these poison arrows coming from beams. Place the flutes at 45-degree angles with the mouthpiece down.

Living Things
Anything that is living has wonderful Chi.

Animals in Feng Shui are referred to as having hot explosive Chi. When I have cleared some Chi in my home, my dog suddenly becomes very excited and runs around in circles.

Animals can also guide us to trouble spots within our surroundings. Friends of mine noticed an abrupt change in their cat's behaviour soon after they moved. Neither cat would leave the bedroom and insisted on staying put day and night. When they showed me around their new home, I came to a corner where the Chi sent a shiver throughout my entire body. As it turned out, the elderly gentlemen who previously occupied the home had kept this corner as a shrine for his dearly departed wife, which included an urn with her ashes, photographs and memorabilia.

We did a Fire Earth Clearing (see the last section of this chapter for details) to remove the negative Chi. Within hours the cats were running and playing happily all over the house.

So do trust your animals: they have a wonderful sense of Chi. Watch to see where they will or will not go in your home. The same holds true of small children.

Plants and trees represent growth and new life. Look to see where plants are flourishing in your home and where they are not. This is indicative of how the Chi is flowing in that Chi Centre. Living plants are vital in cleansing and purifying our environment. The green jade plant resembles the jade stone and as a bonus this plant is considered one of good luck or good fortune and wealth.

Colour
Each colour has a unique energy vibration. Colours are an effective way to change to flow of Chi in any Centre.

Red is the most potent transformative colour in Feng Shui. Red symbolizes Fire and the Chi that promotes change.

The colour red is powerful when used in areas where water is leaving your home, including drainpipes for sinks, toilets and washing machines. Red stops the flow of money leaving your home.

Use red tape along the floor at the entrance to all the bathrooms. If this is not possible, you can place red tape under the doors, which is what I have done in my home. Red tape can be used everywhere you need to fill in a missing piece. You can also use red string or thread to hang your clear crystals. Clear thread should be used instead, however, when hanging colour crystals. Red has a stronger Chi vibration and you don't want red string to overpower the colour of the crystal.

Water
Water creates a wonderful flow of Chi to your space. Water is a Chi attracter and is most beneficial at the front door.

Water features can be placed either on the inside or outside of your home, depending on weather. Flowing water means flowing money. It symbolizes that money not only comes to you but also that your funds are effective and create results.

Resist the temptation to put Water in your Fame and Reputation Chi Centre. The Fame and Reputation Chi Centre is a Fire element and Water douses Fire. You don't want to create a dampening effect on your reputation.

Mirrors
Mirrors act like water too. Because mirrors are reflective, they can be used to expand an area and add extra sunlight to a dim place.

Mirrors are very powerful cures but also can reflect negative Chi. Be sure not to position mirrors in places where they are reflecting something of a negative nature.

When using mirrors for a cure, never use a mirror that is fragmented in several pieces. This distorts the Chi. Always use a quality mirror to expand the entranceway to your home or to reflect back the Chi down a long narrow hallway. Mirrors are also wonderful in the dining room. They double the abundance that is reflected on the table. One caution here, however. Ensure that the mirror's reflection doesn't cut off people's heads when they are sitting at the table.

Hang a mirror above the fireplace if you find there are a lot of family arguments. The fireplace has very strong Fire Chi and the mirror, representing Water, will help bring back balance.

 The Bagua Mirror is also a powerful tool used in Feng Shui. This special eight-sided mirror carries a strong Chi that vibrates the symbol of protection. It provides a very quick and easy cure and a good all rounder for protection and blessing. We would use the Bagua Mirror outdoors above the front door of your home to ward off any negative Chi while enticing positive Chi directed to your home. Always face the mirror away from your home, never facing inwards.

If you have a garage with a room above it, I would suggest that you place a Bagua Mirror on the ceiling of the garage facing down. This will ensure that none of the negative Chi emitting from your car fumes enter the room above.

Use Bagua Mirrors if you have visible electrical lines outside your home. These will deflect the negative Chi. Likewise; you can do the same if there are commercial facilities near your home.

Moving Objects

Hanging mobiles are great for stimulating the Chi. Their swirling movement can create a new flow of Chi, which balances chaotic Chi.

Mobiles are also great for clearing stagnant Chi, especially in those tucked away areas, or to cure sharp edges caused from bookshelves or wall corners. The mobile does not need to be physically moving; it is what it symbolizes that is important.

Mobiles are not the only objects that create this type of Chi. You could use windsocks, flags, banners or pinwheels - virtually anything that moves in the wind. Try putting a Canadian flag somewhere by your front door. The colour Red and the flag's movement create wonderful Chi being attracted through the front door.

Weight

We would generally use weight, such as a piece of heavy furniture, as a cure for a missing piece. The weight symbolizes stability and calm.

Heavy cures are used to emphasize or give form to a missing area.

Use a large heavy bolder to anchor the intersection of the corner of a missing piece. This enhances calmness, stability and security.

You could add a smooth rock to each of the four corners of your children's room like I did, to provide a calm, stable and secure environment for your child.

Fragrance

Our sense of smell is well connected to memory. We can relate to happy or sad times by what we smell. For instance, the smell of turkey can remind us of special times with family at Christmas, or the smell of disinfectant might bring back recollections of a difficult hospital stay.

We can use our sense of smell to stimulate the Chi with incense sticks, fragrant candles, essential oils or even fresh flowers. I like to add a few drops of essential oil to my water fountain; it gives off a wonderful scent when the door is opened and closed.

Fragrance has the ability to change the mood of an environment. Pay close attention to the fragrances and aromas in your environment and notice how they affect your emotions, thoughts and focus. Introducing new scents into your surroundings, like fresh flowers, essential oils, incense, and other pleasant aromas elevate your Chi frequency. By tuning in to fragrance, you will find that your overall sensitivity increases in positive ways.

Eliminating Negative Chi with Space Clearings

Space clearing is a tool used in conjunction with clutter clearing, cleaning and repairs in your home. This type of clearing eliminates the unhealthy Chi that has built up over time. Following the space clearing, the Chi in your space should brighten and circulate more freely and Feng Shui cures will be more effective in this type of environment.

Negative Chi resulting from thoughts, occurrences and stress is absorbed by the walls, furniture, carpet, ceilings and corners. Problems that may have occurred with previous owners or tenants may also impact you in the present. As you have no idea what exactly happened in your home in the past, space clearing allow you to cleanse predecessor's Chi and create clear, positive and auspicious Chi.

Fire Earth Clearing

Supplies:

Ceramic coffee mug, a fire safe place for the mug to stand, Epsom Salts, a new bottle of rubbing alcohol and a wooden match.

Steps:

1. Place the coffee mug in a shallow pan of water.
2. Add three handfuls of Epsom Salts.
3. Add alcohol drops equating to your age plus one extra drop into the mug to cover the salt.
4. Light a match and drop it in the mixture.
5. While the mixture is lit, visualize any negative Chi going into the fire and being transformed into positive Chi or simply being taken away.
6. When the salt burns out, let it cool a bit and throw the mug away.

The Rice Blessing

This beautiful blessing is found in The Learning Annex presents Feng Shui by Meihwa Lin. You can use this blessing if you are moving into a new home or business space. This blessing will cleanse away predecessors' Chi to enable good auspicious Chi to prosper.

Steps:

1. Recite the Heart Calming meditation. (Please refer to page 110 for more details.)

2. Add a pinch of cinnabar powder to uncooked rice then add one drop for each year of your age plus one of alcohol.

3. Mix ingredients with your middle finger on your right hand for female and left for male.

4. Recite The Six True Words mantra (Om Ma Ni Pad Me Hum) as described on page 109 or recite a prayer of your belief, 108 times.

5. Starting at your front door, throw a handful of rice up in the air to uplift the Chi while reciting The Six True Words mantra.

6. Throw another handful outwards. This represents feeding the harmful forces.

7. Throw another handful downwards, again reciting the above mantra. This represents sowing the seeds of a new start.

8. Continue around the perimeter of your space stopping at points where you feel the need to lift the Chi and repeat the previous three steps.

9. Complete the Rice Blessing by performing The Three Secret Reinforcements in Chapter 12.

Chapter 10.
Specific Cures for Specific Issues

I recently consulted with a client whose Relationships and Love Chi Centre was partially missing. When I asked her how things were going with her husband, she teared up almost immediately. She told me the relationship was strained and earlier in the year she had almost left. It confirmed to me that I was dealing with a missing piece rather than a bonus piece. The staircase in her Health Chi Centre also spiralled down from top to bottom. This led me to ask her a question about her family's health. She confided that her whole family had suffered health issues since occupying the space.

Remember that a single cell adapts to its environment. As we are all made up of cells, we also adapt to the Chi all around us. It's important to assess your well-being in each area of your life. If you perceive gaps or disappointments in a specific area, this is an important clue as to where you might begin making changes.

When assessing your home, these are some of the issues you should be looking for:

- Missing pieces
- Interior stairway facing the door
- Front door/back door alignment
- Overhead beams
- Pillars
- Adding a skylight
- Empty door frames
  (representing someone leaving the home)
- Agreeing and Arguing doors

These issues may appear subtle to you but can have quite an effect on your Chi. Fortunately, each is really quite simple to cure.

Let's look at some examples of how you would apply the cures outlined in this chapter to the above situations.

Applying Cures to Missing Pieces
To apply cures to missing pieces, you can add mirrors, plants, crystals, light and red string.

Here are some specific suggestions to expand the missing pieces:

- Use lighting and mirrors both inside and outside your home.
- Add leafy rounded green plants to the two corners of the main walls.
- Hang 30mm crystals, which will deflect the poison arrow from the corner.
- Fill in the area with red string or a line where the wall would have been if it were not missing. Alternately, you can bury a crystal or add three large boulders or shrubs at the point where the two lines should meet. If you have a deck, this naturally fills in the missing piece. Here you can add a planter at the point where the two lines meet or hang a wind chime, flag or windsock.

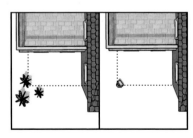 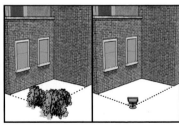

None of these cures are expensive. And you don't have to add all these to make a difference. You may want to add one cure at a time and note any changes before adding the next.

Interior Stairway Facing the Door

It can be problematic when an interior stairway faces the door. This configuration represents your abundance flowing out the door! To counteract this Chi loss, you can add mirrors to either side of the door and hang a 30 to 40 mm crystal between the door and the bottom of the stairs. A red crystal works best, as it is a Chi attracter and kick-starter. Chandeliers also work perfectly in this area.

Front Door/ Back Door Alignment

When the front and back doors to your home are aligned, the Chi comes through the front door and then flows directly out the back door. A cure for this is to place two 40mm crystals evenly spaced between the doors. A wind chime can accomplish the same Chi shift, as can a piece of heavy furniture positioned between the two doors. In any case, these cures redirect the Chi flow to a more beneficial direction.

Overhead Beams

Overhead beams shoot out poison arrows with great force. There are a number of ways to counteract the effects of these poison arrows. For starters, when building a home from scratch have the corners rounded. It's also helpful to paint the beam the same colour as the ceiling.

You can also place two bamboo flutes at 45-degree angles in the middle of the beam or crystals at each corner.

Whenever you enter a room, assess where the beams are and where you may or may not want to sit.

Sloping Beams or Slanted Ceilings

Sloping beams or ceilings represent slow progress in your life. This can be manifested in either mental or physical health problems.

A simple cure for this would be to hang tassels or some kind of fringe that will absorb this negative Chi. Add uplifting lights to lift the Chi back up or add Feng Shui Crystals to rebalance the Chi.

Pillars

Pillars can block the flow of Chi and create four poison arrows. As with overhead beams, creating pillars with rounded corners would be advantageous. Pillars can be transformed several ways: with mirrors on all the sides; or coverings of fabric or silk ivy; or placing plants around the pillar.

I have seen some homes where pillars were made to look like trees and others where pillars were hung with tapestries or banners. You could even hang pictures of flowers or trees around each side.

Skylights

If the skylight was part of the original home design, no cure is necessary. However, adding a skylight in a subsequent renovation is problematic. Symbolically, this represents cutting into the head of the home.

Hang a 30mm crystal in all skylight fixtures added after your home was built. To enhance this cure, choose a crystal colour that matches its corresponding Chi Centre.

Empty Door Frames

Empty door frames occur when a door has been removed but the frame remains standing. This configuration represents someone leaving the home and can be cured by either replacing the door or hanging a curtain in the door frame.

Agreeing versus Arguing Doors

Figure 10.1A and B show examples of doors that are seen to be in agreement.

In figure 10.1A, the doors are the same size and they are in exact alignment.

In figure 10.1B, the doors are completely non-aligned. Because they do not impact each other in any way, however, they are also seen as being in complete agreement. No cures are required for either of these situations.

Figure 10.1C and D highlight situations in which doors are seen to be arguing.

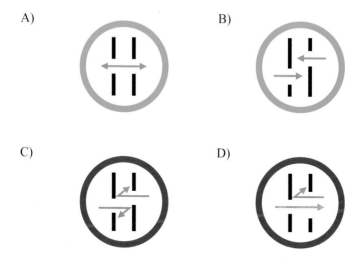

Figure 10.1: Agreeing vs. Arguing Doors

When doors are arguing this causes the Chi to bounce off the opposite wall and creates a tension within the home whereby frustrations or arguments can develop.

Two specific cures can be applied. You can either hang a crystal between the two doors or place convex mirrors at eye level beside each of the doors to show the energy where it needs to go. If these situations pertain to you, apply the cures with the intended outcome in your mind and pay special attention to the changes that you start to experience.

Bathroom Cures

Bathrooms are a huge problem for us. Remembering that water represents money, we lose a great deal of this Chi down the toilet as well as the bathtub, shower and sinks. The same would apply to any exit for water drainage. Of course the bathroom is an important facility that cannot be removed to the back yard, but finding a good location is difficult. Fortunately, in Feng Shui there is always a cure.

A bathroom's location can have unfortunate effects. Here's how bathrooms can work as force reducers in specific Chi Centres:

Prosperity and Wealth Chi Centre: Need I say more! This is where the Chi of your wealth resides and having a bathroom here drains your finances and impedes your ability to attract any abundance in your life.

By The Front Door (Career and Life Path, Skills and Knowledge, or Helpful People and Travel): I list all three Chi Centres because this is how we orientate the Bagua Map. The front entrance is always located in one of these Chi Centres. If the bathroom is situated here or is the first room you see when you enter the space, then all your fresh Chi entering the front door flows directly down the drain. The outcome would be a lack of direction in your life and a downward spiral of your career success.

The Health Chi Centre is one area to avoid at all costs. This Centre relates to your general health, whether physical or mental. This will cause the Chi to deplete in every area of life.

Fame and Reputation is all about your reputation and you certainly do not want this going down the toilet. A good reputation fuels the flames for greatness.

Relationships and Love is not something you want to lose. If we have no love in our life, it manifests into low self-esteem.

This leaves the Family and Foundation and Creativity and Children Chi Centres as the most ideal locations for the bathroom. Regardless of where your bathroom is located on your Bagua map, I still advise you apply the following bathroom cures:

- Always ensure that you keep the toilet lid down. I remember sharing this with my father-in-law. He had this habit of leaving the toilet lid up whenever he came to visit. I advised him that it represented his money Chi flowing down the loo! Since that day forward, the lid has firmly been closed. My mother-in-law was astonished. She shared with me that she had been trying for 50 years to get him to put the lid down.

- Keep the bathroom door closed. It is advisable to reduce the amount of Chi flowing toward the bathroom. Place red on the underside of the door. You can use tape or string or you might even paint the underside of the door.

- Hang a 30mm Feng Shui crystal to the ceiling. This will balance the Chi in this facility.

- Place plants in the bathroom to help drink the dominance of water. These can either be live or silk.

- Place the colour red around the drains leaving the home (i.e., bathroom, kitchen, washing machine) to reduce the amount of Chi from going down the drain.

- When the bathroom is visible from the front door, hang a mirror the full length of the door to reflect the Chi back into the home.

Chapter 11.
The Three Key Chi Centres of the Home

The three key Chi forces in your home include the front door, the kitchen stove and the master bedroom.

These three Chi forces have an enormous impact on your home. They represent how the Chi enters your space and relate to your Relationships and Love and also your abundance in life. I believe that if you have all three balanced then you are in a wonderful position to receive the great benefits the universe has to offer you.

If you decide only to apply these three Feng Shui cures, you will see a significant difference in the Chi force within your home.

Front Door
I like to think of the front door as the ambassador to your home. This is where the Chi enters your space and nourishes the rest of your home.

I often hear clients say, "We never use the front door; we always come in from the garage." It makes no difference. The front door is the main entrance that the architect designed it to be. No matter where you physically enter your home, the front door on your floor plan is where the Chi force enters in. Open your front door at least once a day.

Remember, when laying the Bagua Map on your floor plan, the front door will fall in either the Skills and Knowledge, Career and Life Path, or Helpful People and Travel Chi Centres. There are a number of ways of attracting Chi and one is to paint your front door any shade of red, including burgundy, orange or brown. The colour red is a Fire colour and a Chi attracter. If you do not want to repaint your door, then you could add a doormat, flag or windsock with red in its colour scheme.

I like to add vibrant red flowers in cast iron containers. During the winter months, I fill the containers with silk flowers instead. Poinsettias are beautiful for the winter months and look very festive. Water fountains either inside or outside the door are just great. Wind chimes are beautiful sound attracters, bringing wonderful Chi to your home.

Ensure that your front door is well lit. Bright light attracts positive Chi. Your front door area should also be clean and clear of clutter. Quickly dispose of junk mail and clear away anything that inhibits access.

I am often asked how to raise the energy of the home. My first question is, "What do you have both outside and inside the front door or entrance? Is there anything there that is cluttering the space?" The response is always the same - too much stuff and clutter. When we have clutter here it inhibits the "Mouth of Chi" from achieving sustenance to enhance the rest of the home or space.

Kitchen Stove
The kitchen stove signifies your source of food and your continuing ability to get enough food. This area represents your abundance in all ways.

To get the Chi flowing:

- Make sure the stove is clean - inside and out. This applies to everything used to cook food including the barbeque, microwave and toaster. Make sure the burners are all working and you use them equally.
- Place a mirror behind your stove if it is against the wall. This helps to make the cook feel less vulnerable and symbolically doubles the abundance.
- Hang a crystal above the microwave to absorb its EMF.

You will also need to watch for a Fire/Water conflict. (Remember, Water reduces Fire.) To avoid this, make sure that your stove does not align with the refrigerator, sink or dishwasher. Also ensure that there is no Water conflict on the other side of the wall such as the washing machine or bathroom. If this situation can't be avoided, you will need to add the Wood Element such as the colour green between them. For instance, you could use a rug or a plant. In my case, I've taped a large piece of green card to the wall behind my washing machine. Do ensure that you do not put card by the stove though; we do not want to cause a fire hazard!

Remember the building cycle: Water feeds Wood and Wood fuels Fire. Without the element Wood, Water puts out Fire. Simply, by adding the element Wood you turn a conflict into a positive. If you have a bathroom above your kitchen, you can paint your ceiling green or place a large green mat on the floor of the bathroom room above.

The Master Bedroom
The bedroom is not only a place to get a good night's sleep, but it also shelters and comforts you. This is where your romantic love manifests itself and is a special place to recharge your Chi.

Some people struggle with the idea of not having a television in their bedroom. If you are to truly recharge, then peace and tranquillity are essential. Television, as entertaining and informative as it can be, will interfere with your ability to relax and connect with spirit. Think of spiritual retreats or spa visits. You will never find a television in the room. Proprietors want to be sure there is nothing to distract you from attaining total relaxation.

We treat the bedroom as a Relationships and Love Chi Centre, regardless of where it may fall on the Bagua map. The master bedroom is where the parents should always sleep. This is the only Chi Centre where things are arranged in pairs to symbolize a union. Everywhere else you work with triads. In this room, position everything in pairs, including night stands and lamps.

We all have different ideas on how a romantic bedroom should look. Imagine a bedroom in a fancy hotel - I mean a really expensive hotel. What would you expect to see in the bedroom? Why not recreate that room and have all the luxuries you desire. You deserve it!

Ensure that you sleep on a bed that is made of wood. Metal beds have vibrating, clanging Chi and will keep you up in the night. King size beds are really two twin-sized beds put together. In Feng Shui terms, this creates barriers between you and your partner. To attract a partner or to keep the Chi strong between you and your partner, sleep on a queen- or double-sized bed. The Chi can flow more freely if there is nothing under the bed, so be sure to remove all clutter. If you do have a king, you could place a red sheet between the box spring and mattress. There is always a cure.

In Feng Shui it is advisable to either replace the bed or at a minimum change the mattress after a death, serious illness or divorce. Chi resides in everything and even when a person dies, or leaves a space, their residual Chi remains in their belongings. Sadly, I've witnessed examples of this within my own family.

A few years ago, my sister returned from another country to live with my mum in the United Kingdom. This was a particularly hard time for her, as life had not turned out as she'd hoped.

She moved into the bedroom that once belonged to my late father. There were still many of my father's items scattered about, including his false teeth! Other personal belongings like his favourite sweater, hat and walking stick continued to reside in the room. As did his bed. Imagine the negative Chi dwelling there.

My sister lived in this situation for several months. She was not doing well, suffering health issues and unable to sleep. It was not until she replaced the bed and removed all of my father's belongings that things started to improve. Directly after, she reported her best night's sleep in six months.

Your budget might not always allow you to replace the bed or mattress. Fortunately in Feng Shui, there is always a cure. Before using a second-hand mattress, place it outside in direct sunlight for at least nine hours. Then wave sandalwood incense around the mattress before bringing it back inside.

Another important consideration is the bed's positioning. Always try and place your bed in the command position. Think of a 'Mafia' guy in a restaurant. He chooses to sit at the back of the room with his back to a solid wall. Here he can see the door and feel protected. Now imagine your bed in this position. Would you not feel more relaxed and secure and better able to get a good night's rest?

Place the bed as far as possible from the door; make sure you can see most of the room from the bed - particularly the bedroom door. Your headboard should be against a solid wall. Make sure your feet are not facing directly out of the door when you are lying on your bed. Ancient Chinese considered this the death position! Your feet should not face the bathroom door either. If this is the case, then place a 30mm crystal on the ceiling at the mid-point from the foot of the bed to the bathroom door. This will redirect Chi and protect you.

Having a door leaving the bedroom to the outside of the home represents one of you leaving the relationship. This situation can be cured with either a crystal hung above the door or a wind chime to redirect the Chi.

Remove any mirrors from the bedroom. When you sleep, your body and mind are processing the energies of the day and your spirit leaves your body. If you have a mirror, especially on the wall opposite the bed, your spirit will be reflected in the mirror and will reflect back at your body with great force, targeting poison arrows. If it is not possible to remove the mirror, at least cover it over when you sleep.

Hang pictures or photographs of a romantic nature. Your bedroom is not the place for photographs of your family or children. (These should be placed in your Family and Foundation or Creativity and Children Centres instead.) Your wedding photographs (more than three years old) should not be in here either. Instead, use recent photographs of you and your partner to keep the Chi fresh.

Placing fresh flowers in your bedroom once a week will lift the Chi. I have been on many consultations where dried bridal bouquets are displayed. Dried flowers or potpourri are dead negative Chi and should be removed from the home.

Only keep the book that you are reading next to your bed. Read relaxing novels and avoid reading the newspaper before going to sleep. Imagine the negative Chi you read in the newspapers. You do not want to sleep having this negativity in your mind.

Add two pieces of rose quartz to your room or a pink crystal to your room. They bring very positive Chi in the bedroom.

Extra Tips for Children's Bedrooms
Ensure that your child sleeps on a bed that is made primarily of wood. Metal is a clanging Chi and your child will not sleep well. Avoid spindles or shelves above your child's head, as these cause shooting arrows.

I would recommend new beds for each of your children. Remember, second-hand beds keep the previous occupant's Chi. If the bed belonged to someone else, then that person's Chi is residing there, too. If it is not possible to change the bed then you could do a space clearing on the bed.

Place the bed in the command position against a solid wall with no windows. Ensure your child can see the door in order to feel safe and secure.

Choosing yin colours for the room will promote relaxation. Avoid primary, bright colours. Colour has Chi too. I remember my daughter insisting on having a red room. Her temper rose too! Good colours for children are green for growth, blue for calming spiritual Chi, purple or lavender for self esteem, pink for good relationships, white for creativity and communication, and soft yellow for balance, health and grounding.

Remove TVs and computers from your child's room. Electrical equipment creates too much Chi, which will disturb your child's sleep and create mood swings and a lack of concentration. If it is not possible to remove these items at least cover them over at night and pull out the plug. Even the electric clock and bedside light can have a negative effect on your child. Ensure that the wires are not touching the bed and that they are not too close to your child's head. You could put a small Salt Crystal lamp between the wires and your child. This will absorb some of the negative Chi.

Chapter 12.
Adding Power with the
"Three Secret Reinforcements"

Once you have completed your mundane cures and changes to your space it is important to add the "Three Secret Reinforcements". The Professor states that when you make any physical or mundane changes to your space, without adding the power of the Three Secret Reinforcements, your results are likely to be very weak.

These Reinforcements are known as "transcendental cures" and are extremely sacred teachings in BTB Feng Shui. They are honoured and treated in a highly respectful way.

Using body, mind and speech you are adding power to your Feng Shui adjustments. They become intensified and send out a clear message of your intentions. His Holiness Grandmaster Professor Lin Yun teaches us that when we make the mundane changes or physical cures, these only account for 30% of the end result. The remaining 70% is brought about by your belief and intention, your power of prayer and visualization.

When beginning this ritual it is very important to understand how the body, mind and speech work and how we implement the blessing to its full potential.

Body Chi
First, the body Chi is a gesture using the hands. In other words, we call this a mudra, a silent gesture of the body. We in the West are quite comfortable using the hand to introduce ourselves; we shake hands to express friendship. Applying the mudra is simply gesturing our intentions.

Here are two methods I would like to share for expressing the mudra in BTB Feng Shui.

Ousting Mudra

Use your middle and third finger bent with your thumb covering their nails. Leaving your index and little finger raised, flick the two bent fingers outwards to expel the harmful Chi. You may substitute a personal spiritual tradition for this mudra.

Heart Sutra Mudra

With your palms facing upwards, place your left hand on top of your right hand, with your middle fingers lining up together. Then cup your hands, like you are holding a ball, and gently touch your thumbs together. Lower your hands so they are placed approximately two inches below your navel.

Mind

The mind aspect of the Three Secret Reinforcements is the most important of the three. We use our mind to visualize our intentions.

When planning a dance routine, for example, you might start by visualizing a scenario from a movie. In your mind, you will visualize every step of the dance, from gliding onto the floor through to the final bow.

When applying the mind aspect of the Three Secret Reinforcements, keep a clear image in your mind of your intended goal.

Speech

When we add speech to the blessing, we are adding powerful sacred sounds to initiate the power of the spoken word. These are called mantras. A mantra, which is also referred to as a prayer, is a group of words pulled together and recited repetitiously. There are several mantras used in BTB Feng Shui, and I have listed two here. Feel free to recite your own personal prayer relevant to your own spiritual belief system.

The Six True Words Mantra:

Om Ma Ni Pad Me Hum

Roughly translated, this means:

I bow to the jewel in the lotus blossom or I see the God within you and I acknowledge and bow to that light.

We call upon the power of compassion with this mantra, which uplifts our Chi to increase personal luck.

The Heart Sutra
(otherwise known as Heart Calming Mantra)

Gate, Gate (gah-tay, gah-tay)
Para, gate (pair-uh gah-tay)
Para sum gate (pair-uh sum gah-tay)
Bodhi swaha (boh-dee swa-ha)

Roughly translated, the Heart Sutra means:

Go or run (Gate, Gate)
to the other side of the shore or nirvana, (Para gate)
many, or numerous, times, (Para sum gate)
being aware of all truths, knowing all things and
having wisdom and omni-science, and do so quickly
(Bodhi swaha)

This powerful mantra improves your personal Chi
and is especially useful if you are feeling uneasy
or fearful. It raises your Chi vibration and invokes
the power of peace and calmness while clearing all
negativity that surrounds you.

Red Envelope Tradition

The ritual of the Red Envelope Tradition is a way to honour and respect the sacred Feng Shui information that has been given. You are participating in a sacred ritual that has been passed down by generations of Feng Shui Masters who have shared their knowledge with us. By performing this tradition, you are harnessing the wisdom of the ancients, empowering the specific cures.

The colour red symbolizes good fortune and its positive Chi and power will dissolve any negative Chi. The rectangle shape of the envelope symbolizes protection and is the same shape as ancient shields of protection. Symbolically, both the receiver and giver are being protected from bad Chi.

When transcendental cures are shared, it is the tradition in BTB Feng Shui to receive at least one or multiples of three Red Envelopes. Usually, nine Red Envelopes are given, depending on how many cures are offered. The Red Envelopes offer protection and continued good luck to individuals who have parted with sacred information they have received from honoured and respected masters. When this tradition is complied with, the receiver of the envelope should place it under a pillow after performing the Three Secret Reinforcements. Disposal of the contents is entirely your choice, however, the Red Envelope should not be used again for the purpose of this tradition.

Envelopes can simply be kept for the New Year or Chinese New Year and then burned. When burning, you will visualize sending all the positive abundance received throughout the year back to the universe. Remember that what you give, you receive back two fold. Another way of disposing of the envelopes is to donate them to a local kindergarten or scrapbooking establishment for decoration purposes.

Chapter 13.
Designing a Floor Plan

If you are fortunate enough to be involved in the design process of your home, these suggestions will definitely benefit you.

Try to keep the front of your home (i.e., Skills and Knowledge, Career and Life Path, and Helpful People and Travel Chi Centres) for your family/living room and study/office. These rooms benefit from the auspicious Chi that enters the front door and therefore enhances your career, social activities and family get-togethers.

Placing your children's bedrooms towards the front section of the home will enhance their development into healthy confident citizens. If this is not possible then hang a 30mm Feng Shui Crystal in the centre of the bedroom ceiling to reflect the Chi to the opposite side of the home.

When thinking of rooms for the rear of the home, I would suggest a kitchen in the Fame and Reputation area. Fame and Reputation is a Fire Element. The hot stove would definitely heat up this Centre by stoking the flames of great fortune. Secure your reputation by ensuring that the stove cannot be seen from the front door, regardless of where the stove falls on the Bagua Map.

Position the master bedroom in the Relationships and Love Chi Centre and the dining room in the Prosperity and Wealth Chi Centre. I would also enhance the Chi of the dining room by placing a mirror on the wall opposite the table to reflect the abundance of that being served. Ensure that the head of the tallest person at the table is not cut off when reflected in the mirror. Again, if it is not possible to place these rooms here and you find they fall in the front areas of the home, hang a Feng Shui Crystal in the centre of the respective ceiling. If a Feng Shui Crystal does not fit your décor then hang a mirror on the opposite side of the house to reverse the image.

Now we have covered the front and rear sections of your home, let's focus on the Health Chi Centre. The Chi Centre relates to your general health, whether this is mental or physical, so it is a very important Chi Centre to protect.

This is one area of the home where I suggest you avoid storage. Ideally keep this Chi Centre open and clear of any blockages. Keep the Chi flowing smoothly without having furniture weighing it down.

Avoid having the staircase in the Health Chi Centre as well. The spiralling Chi pulls down many aspects of your life, including opportunities, career success and health.

A client of mine, as well as all members of her family, had been experiencing severe illness since occupying their home. Unfortunately, her staircase was located in the centre of the home. A cure for this situation is to hang a large Feng Shui Crystal, as large as your budget permits and preferably yellow in colour, on the ceiling above the staircase. For double measure, I would suggest placing nine healthy green rounded leaf plants along the staircase. If live plants are not an option, apply a silk vine to the banister.

The Health Chi Centre is not a good place for your kitchen. The hot Chi is too much and can create health issues, not to mention a fire hazard. Either hang a Feng Shui crystal above the stove to protect the cook or hang a mirror in the rear of the home as mentioned above.

Safeguard your healthy relationships by keeping your bedroom out of the Health Chi Centre. The vibrant Chi here will keep you awake at night, cause arguments between you and your partner, and create other health issues, including mental confusion. Cure this problem with the mirror cure, as described above, or hang a Feng Shui crystal above the bed.

Figure 13.1 Floor Plan Summary

Area	Force Builders	Force Reducers
Rear of Home	Kitchen Master Bedroom	Family/Living Room Study/Office Children/Guest Rooms
Centre of Home	Free Space in Health Chi Centre	Storage in Health Chi Centre Staircase Kitchen Master Bedroom
Front of Home	Family/Living Room Study/Office Children/Guest Rooms	Kitchen Master Bedroom Dining Room

Chapter 14.
Clearing Your Clutter

Clutter can be anything that is not needed or loved - something that does not make you feel good; things that are untidy or disorganised; too many things in too small a space; and anything unfinished.

You would never consider dancing in an establishment where the floor is covered in debris. Most of us expect a clean and tidy space where we work or play. Yet, too often, we don't set the same standards within our homes and end up living in a space filled with clutter.

When we lay the Bagua Map over our space, we come to realize that clutter areas do have a direct impact on our lives. The nine Chi Centres represent every area of our lives. Accumulating clutter in these Chi Centres causes blocked Chi and results in an imbalance in our personal Chi. When we remove clutter, we will release this blocked Chi and make a shift that creates changes in our lives very quickly.

Let's look at how clutter in any of the Chi Centres affects your life:

Prosperity and Wealth
Clutter here has a real effect on our personal finances and all the abundance in our lives, including an abundance of health, wealth and happiness.

Fame and Reputation
Our personal reputations and how others perceive us are affected here. Too much blocked Chi in the Fame and Reputation area affects popularity and tarnishes self-esteem.

Relationships and Love
Do we really need to go here? We never want to block the very important Chi Centre of Love! This can cause difficulties in finding a partner and improving relationships with an existing partner. And not

just relationships in a romantic nature are compromised. Clutter can also have negative consequences on our relationships with business associates, children and friends.

Creativity and Children
Clutter in this area can have many negative consequences. When Chi is blocked here, life may not feel joyful. We may have difficulties completing projects or communicating with our children and others. Even difficulties in conceiving children can be tracked back to here.

Helpful People and Travel
Why can I never find people to help me when I need them? Why is planning a trip so difficult? Blocked Chi in this area is likely the culprit.

Career and Life Path
When life appears to be in slow motion and the dance is becoming exhausting, Chi is struggling in this Chi Centre.

Skills and Knowledge
Clutter in this area makes learning those new dance routines so difficult. Whatever move we make to improve ourselves, we feel like we're tripping over our feet. When Chi is blocked in this area, our ability to learn new skills is inhibited.

Family and Foundation
Clutter in this area results in squabbles and discontent. Family dynamics are affected by blocked Chi here.

Health
Blocks here cause bad Chi to erode our physical and mental health.

Removing the Blocked Chi
We are a society of hoarders and we love any excuse to keep hold of the "stuff" in our lives. Many people believe that they are judged by the quantity versus the quality of their possessions. Dancing with baggage makes the whole experience very tiring; we soon become disinterested and exhausted by the routine. The story of clutter is that it brings with it a very negative Chi. To bring positive changes into our lives we must de-clutter our space first and then implement Feng Shui cures.

Remember, too much clutter in life manifests into struggles. When considering blocked Chi, think of it as a very dense dark Chi that has a sticky dark substance to it. Imagine dancing in mud, where the going is difficult and slow. Who wouldn't feel tired and lethargic? Clearing away the debris also clears away the sluggishness while we attempt to make change, and then the dance is a breeze. We find our lives opening up to new opportunities and good things beginning to present themselves to us.

One of the most damaging consequences of holding onto clutter is its tendency to keep us in the past. As you start sifting through boxes, drawers and closets, emotions that have been buried for years can start flooding to the surface. There is an enormous amount of negative Chi in this emotional clutter. Only by letting go of our "stuff" - both physically and emotionally - can we free the blocked Chi.

This certainly applies to our thoughts too. Our inner chatter has a great impact on our lives. I'm talking about that little voice in your head. The one that warns you against doing something - just in case you make a fool of yourself. It's the same voice that chastises you for not achieving more - the one that tries to boost your sense of worth by judging people and situations harshly. These thoughts too must go.

So where do you start in the process of clearing clutter? First try to understand what is missing in your life. For most, this is related to health, wealth and happiness. Take a look at the dance floor of your life. What is most important to you? What do you wish you had more of? These are the areas to focus on first. Removing blockages in our Chi Centres opens us up to opportunities in life. It is only then that we realize the dance is easily manoeuvred and the process enjoyable.

Chapter 15.
Feng Shui Abundance Winners

As a Feng Shui Teacher, I have been blessed to work with a wonderful array of students from all walks of life. So many have chosen to use Feng Shui as a method to take control and responsibility for their lives and well-being. Here are a few of their stories.

Improving Health and Family Relationships

One student who attended my class was looking for ways to help improve her son's health as well as her marital and family relationships. When I visited her home, I found her staircase located in the centre of her house and her family portraits displayed along the staircase wall. The Chi from the staircase was being pulled down in a spiralling fashion and, therefore, draining away the good Chi from each family member. I also found that their beloved family pet's ashes were also being stored in this area. Anything that is dead - from dried flowers to the remains of a loved one or family pet - has a strong negative Chi and will draw the entire auspicious Chi within it. Eventually, this works to pull the positive Chi to a negative result. It was no surprise to me that the family dynamics, romantic relationships and health were being affected here. I also found that the husband's office was placed in the Family and Foundation Chi Centre of the home. This room was very disorganized with paper and clutter filling the floor space as well as the desk.

My first suggestion was to remove the remains of the family pet and put them to rest in a more appropriate setting. The remains could be scattered in a flowing river or ocean or buried in consecrated ground designated for animals. Second, I suggested she remove the family portraits from around the staircase and replace them with beautiful potted plants. This reduces the amount of Chi funnelling downward. I also suggested she should organize and reduce the clutter in the office.

A month after implementing the changes, the student reported that relationships with her husband had improved immensely. The family had experienced a wonderful festive holiday season together. Their son's health was starting to improve and he was making progress towards his recovery.

Finding a Perfect Partner

A student decided to take my Feng Shui class to see if she could change the Chi and find the perfect partner to share her life with. She had been longing for romance for more than 10 years. I discovered she was keeping clothing and memorabilia from a previous relationship in her bedroom, which is her Relationships and Love Chi Centre. Keeping items from a previous relationship is not conducive to attracting another, as the former partner's Chi remains in the space. I suggested she remove these items and improve the space with Feng Shui enhancements. She gladly acted on my advice. At the following class she happily announced, "I've met someone over the Internet." Four months later she was married. She also applied Feng Shui cures to help sell her home within one day of listing it on the market.

Bringing Prosperity and Fame to a Campaign Office

I like to introduce homework for my students so they can get to work on their space and improve the Chi for life enhancement. One student decided to offer her services to a last minute candidate who was running for office in the local government. She worked on his campaign office to bring Prosperity, Wealth and Fame. The candidate did indeed successfully win his place. Now a convert, he decided to work on his new office space at City Hall. Being the last member in, choices of offices was down to one. You got it - his space was the worst of the lot. After applying Feng Shui cures, he found that everyone complimented him on how wonderful the space felt, and his future is progressing brilliantly.

Getting a Good Night's Sleep

Sleeping is a problem for so many. But often, sleep issues can be simply cured by addressing the position of the bed in relation to the door and window. One student complained that she'd not had a good night's sleep since occupying her new home. Space was limited as her bedroom was quite small, so she had placed her bed against an interior wall with the television on the other side. This meant she did not have a clear view of the door. In Feng Shui, we like to be in a position of "Command". After convincing her to change the room around, the student returned to class and announced she was having the best sleep ever.

Letting Go

Keeping hold of the past is tough for people to let go of. When we realize that everything has a Chi of its own and that it can either nourish or deplete our personal Chi, we can make the changes necessary to move forward. A student of mine had experienced the loss of a very close sister and had chosen to keep her sister's personal belongings underneath her bed. My student's Chi was very low and emitted anger, pain and grief. After completing the class she went about letting go of all her sister's belongings. This was precisely what was needed to shift her personal Chi. The transformation I witnessed was breathtaking. She had lost the excess weight she had gained through the experience. Her anger had been replaced with love, her pain with joy, and her grief with optimism.

Turning Business Around

A client of mine was having difficulties in her real estate practice. She had been suffering great losses of business, which was surprising since, at the time, the property market was booming. On observing her office floor space, she noted that her stockroom and bathrooms were situated in the Prosperity and Wealth section of the Bagua Map. The stockroom was filled to the brim with files, out-of-date literature, a telephone system about 20 years old, computer parts and boxes of stationary. These were all stored on a floor-to-ceiling shelving unit, with every square inch used. And you took your life in your hands when using the bathroom facilities. The bathrooms were grimy in décor, the toilets had no lid and were insecure, the washbasin was cracked, and the faucet leaked. This was a huge indicator that she was losing money. And she was losing money fast.

After acting on my recommendations to clear clutter and add bathroom cures, she successfully turned her business around and is experiencing great success.

Missing Pieces

One student of mine has had a particularly life-altering experience with Feng Shui. Here is her story, shared in her own words:

"In the beginning, I believed that a long procession of all too many coincidences had delivered me to Feng Shui. When I found myself in Dawn's class, 'Clear Your Clutter through Feng Shui', she and her husband taught me that there were no coincidences but rather an energetic pathway of events that were guiding me as I followed my intuitions appropriately.

When I attended Dawn's class, my world was literally crumbling around me. Only months earlier, I thought I had the perfect life. I was in love with my husband and we were trying to start a family. I had certainly not been conscious of anything amiss.

I still recall her gasp the first time I shared my floor plans. Dawn immediately understood that I was in fact missing pieces in my Prosperity and Wealth, Fame and Reputation, and Relationships and Love Chi Centres and that my stairway was situated right in the middle of my home in the Health Chi Centre.

She inquired about these particular areas of my life, which unbeknownst to her were very difficult and painful for me to expose. My intuition had brought me to Feng Shui and to this woman, and it was then I decided to turn my attention to this new voice of mine and trust it once again. A part of me was hesitant to open up to this complete stranger, yet I was grateful for her seemingly genuine interest.

I began to share my story. My husband had had an affair. After learning of his unfaithfulness, I had fallen down the stairs and fractured several vertebrates in my spine. We had since separated and he had taken my dog, yet routinely visited our home each day. My injury and illness resulted in a diagnosis of Major Depressive Disorder (MDD). I could no longer work and was experiencing extreme issues with both my employer and insurance company. It felt like my once strong self esteem and confidence had vanished overnight, and I was struggling with daily thoughts of departing this earth.

As I began to share with Dawn, further health issues and memories sprang to mind. Since living in this particular house, my husband had developed and survived thyroid cancer and my beloved pet dog had developed a tumour and was now afflicted with Cushing's Disease. And we had not been successful in conceiving a child.

Dawn offered me Feng Shui cures and advice and I took these teachings to heart and really went to work. We laid the Bagua map over the entire floor plan, and she made suggestions to address the missing pieces and the stairway. I hung a 50mm crystal from the second story ceiling directly above the stairway and entwined silk ivy vines through the stairway's spindles. I hung crystals and used both mirrors and plants inside the house to fill in the missing pieces. The outside pieces were filled in with the use of solar lights, stones and red string buried along lines of the missing walls. I then reviewed each zone and the way the elements interacted with one another. I cleared clutter, reviewed storage areas, cleaned and made repairs in every area of the entire house and started the work of setting intentions for each area of my life and its applicable zone.

Dawn told me that next I needed to start the Chi flowing and to start with the three most important areas of the home - the front door, stove and master bedroom. I cleaned my front door, replaced the doorknob, added a brass kick plate and hung a red silk rose wreath and a Bagua Mirror. In the inside entrance I added a mirror, water fountain, a 50mm crystal and a decorative mat. I made a habit of opening this door wide each morning to welcome in the Chi. I cleaned my stove, replaced the burner inserts, put a mirror against the wall behind it and hung 30mm crystals over the cooking surface and above the microwave. I replaced our king-size bed with a queen and added linens in a cranberry colour. A Bagua map was laid beneath the mattress and all was removed from under the bed.

I started using aromatherapy and applied cures, colours and elements for each zone. I performed all of the drain cures, found a silver box, added water fountains, added shelf paper to drawers and cupboards, moved TVs and rearranged the furniture and artwork. I purchased salt crystal lamps, added both Bagua Mirrors and maps and performed the 'Three Secret Reinforcements' blessing with each change. I followed Dawn's advice along with other Feng Shui Teachers and Practitioners, who were now being attracted into my life. They have not only assisted me with this entire process but have become great friends.

The energy in the house changed so much. After months of a stalled life, things began to happen, and happen fast. As Dawn instructed, I hung a red crystal in my Life Path. A week later, my spouse told me he wanted a divorce and later sued me for just that. The divorce settlement agreement then forced me to leave my home. At the same time, my Disability Insurance Appeal was finally approved, and I had the support and financial assistance to find a new home and move. New people, perfect strangers and healthcare providers, came into my life at times when I needed help most, providing assistance, support and friendship. Resources, workshops, books, DVDs began appearing, and a whole new world has opened up to me for which I will be forever grateful. My only regret is that I had not been aware of this knowledge before my life completely fell apart. Feng Shui did not work in the way I had envisioned, but it did in fact create much-needed change. Dawn has made me a believer and I look forward to life's continuing adventure as I use this knowledge of Feng Shui in my new home and life."

Chinese Symbol for Gratitude

Last Word

My hope is that this book will inspire you to take control of your dance of life. I have found that my dance shoes have not stopped tapping the floor to life's beat. I feel I've been gliding effortlessly across the dance floor since applying the simple and precise principles of Feng Shui. Keeping the Chi moving and adjusting the course of your step will help you to experience the beauty of your life's journey.

Enjoy the dance, every step of the way.

With warmest wishes and gratitude,

Dawn

Glossary

Bagua Map
A tool used in BTB Feng Shui to orientate the flow of Chi towards the centre. The centre represents our Chi returning to source. Orientation of the map is made by identifying the front door within one of the following Chi Centres: Skills and Knowledge; Career and Life Path; or Helpful People and Travel.

Bamboo Flute
A musical instrument, used in Feng Shui as a cure. The base of the flute is the root with the space between the joints growing bigger. This demonstrates support and raising of the Chi so life is better than yesterday and improving tomorrow.

BTB Feng Shui
Black Sect Tantric Buddhist Feng Shui - also referred to as Black Hat. Having roots in pre-Buddhist, Bon religion of Tibet. With influences of Indian Buddhism and Chinese philosophy, BTB Feng Shui was introduced to the West by HH Grandmaster Professor Lin Yun in 1980.

Chi
Energy or life force.

Clutter
A blockage of Chi. A stagnation of Chi or energy.

Crystals
Amplifiers or transmitters of Chi. Used in Feng Shui as a remedy.

Cure
An action to achieve balance and harmony.

EMF - Electromagnetic Field
An electrical flow of energy.

Elements
Fire, Earth, Metal, Water and Wood. Natural components of
this planet.

Energy
Chi or life force.

Feng
Chinese translation for Wind or Air.

Feng Shui
Chinese translation for Wind and Water.

Feng Shui Consultant or Practitioner
A trained professional offering services or teachings in this
ancient art.

Heart Calming Mantra
A recital of words to improve the Chi and calm the heart and mind
"Gate, gate, para gate, para som gate, Bodhi Swahha'.

Mantra
A sacred chant of prayers to induce an altered state
of consciousness.

Mouth of Chi
The front entrance where the Chi enters a space.

Mudra
A hand gesture used for blessings.

Mundane Cure
A physical application.

Poison Arrow - Also known as 'Sha Chi' or 'Secret Arrow'
Cutting Chi from a negative or harmful corner or stagnant Chi such as beams, trusses and unfortunate establishments such as funeral homes or cemeteries.

Red Envelope Tradition
An exchange of red envelopes containing money between a client or student to a practitioner or teacher who has provided transcendental cures.

Shui
Chinese translation for Water.

Space Clearing
A method used to clear negative Chi from a space.

Three Secret Reinforcements
A transcendental ritual to raise the effectiveness of a cure using the body, mind and speech.

Trigram
Symbols representing each of the Chi Centres of the Bagua. These symbols indicate three horizontal straight or broken lines read from the bottom up. The bottom line represents the Earth, the middle represents Man, and the top represents Heaven.

Yang
The opposite of Yin. Symbolizes light, movement and masculine.

Yin
The opposite of Yang. Symbolizes dark, stillness and feminine.

REFERENCES

Clear Your Clutter with Feng Shui by Karen Kingston

Feng Shui and Health - The Anatomy of a Home
by Nancy SantoPietro

Feng Shui Bible by Simon Brown

Feng Shui Book for Kids and Their Parents
by Selina Crystal L. Jan

Feng Shui for Dummies by David Kennedy

Feng Shui Revealed by R.D. Chin

In The Feng Shui Zone by Debra Ford

Interior Design with Feng Shui by Sarah Rossbach

The Learning Annex Presents Feng Shui by Meihwa Lin

INTERNET RESOURCES

www.imnalagroup.ca

www.yunlintemple.org

www.ifsguild.org

www.feng-shui-institute.org

www.fengshuimarket.ca

www.katherinemetz.com

www.eileenweklar.com

www.fengshuishopper.com

www.radiantchi.com

INDEX OF FIGURES AND EXERCISES

INDEX

junk, 100

karma, xiii
key, 33, 57, 72, 88, 99
kidneys, 46
kitchen, xiii, 97, 99, 100-1, 113-5
knife, 45
knowledge, 20, 33, 35-6, 44, 63-4, 82, 96, 99, 111, 113, 118, 126, 131

landscapes, 44, 62
library, 64, 74
life, xi, xiii, 17-19, 23, 25, 27-30, 33-6, 38, 41, 44, 46-7, 51, 53, 55-6, 59, 60-4, 68-9, 71-3, 77-9, 81-3, 91, 94, 96-7, 99, 103, 113-4, 117-120, 121-6, 129, 131-2
light(s), 27-8, 40, 43, 54, 78-81, 85, 92, 94, 100, 105, 109, 125, 133
lighting, 78, 92
liver, 47
living things, 79, 83
longevity, xiii
lot, 79, 122
luck, xiii, 75, 84, 109, 111
lungs, 45

magic, 74
Mantra(s), xiv, 90, 109, 132
meditation, 20, 29, 71, 90
metal element, 45, 48-50, 52, 57-9, 62, 66, 102, 105
mind, 17, 28, 57, 64, 72, 88, 98, 104, 107, 109, 125, 132-3
mirror(s), 24, 40, 46, 54-5, 61-2, 85-6, 92-4, 96-7, 100-1, 104, 113-4, 125-6
missing pieces, 38-40, 85, 87, 91-2, 120, 124-5
mobiles, 87
money, xii, 17, 38, 46, 52, 61, 78, 81, 85, 96-7, 123, 133
moon, 27
mountains, 30, 43-4, 62, 75
mouth, 35, 45, 72, 100, 132

佛

DAWN
HANKINS

渡有緣

己丑端午承黑敷再傳人

女法王覓立仁波切雅屬

沐浴焚香持毎量咒　書為作者

暨讀者闔府長幼祈福納吉添壽進財

保平安

雲林禪寺

寺禪

林雲　時客覓立
紫虹軒

About the Author

Dawn Hankins is an accomplished Feng Shui consultant who has dedicated her Feng Shui career to assist individuals, businesses and organizations with life changing transformations. Her studies with His Holiness Grandmaster Professor Lin Yun have been the impetus to becoming a successful Feng Shui consultant, published author; and host of the *Feng Shui Today* television series. In addition to being a popular instructor for the Feng Shui Practitioner Certificate Programme at Mount Royal University, Dawn develops and teaches customized classes for schools and corporations locally and internationally. An expert in her field, she is a sought after guest speaker for a wide variety of organizations, and she offers a vibrant mentorship programme to Feng Shui students. For more information on guest speaking engagements, custom workshops, and private home or business consultations, please contact Dawn Hankins at www.imnalagroup.ca.

Dawn Hankins
Tel No. (403) 619-1812
Email: dawn.hankins@imnalagroup.ca
www.imnalagroup.ca

IMNALA GROUP